College Reading Sk...

Selections from the Black, Book One
Provocative Selections by Black Writers
Third Edition

Edward Spargo, Editor

Consultant for Editorial Content:
Barry Beckham
Associate Professor of English
Brown University

Consultant for Instructional Design:
Mary Prosser Rynn
Staff Developer
New York City Public Schools

Books in the Series:
Book One   Book Three
Book Two   Book Four

 Jamestown Publishers

Selections from the Black, Book One

Third Edition

Catalog No. 821
Copyright © 1989 by Jamestown Publishers, Inc., a
division of NTC/Contemporary Publishing Company,
4255 West Touhy Avenue, Lincolnwood (Chicago),
Illinois, 60646-1975, U.S.A.

Cover and text design by Deborah Hulsey Christie

Cover credit: Anonymous Owner. Photograph courtesy of
Museum of Art, Rhode Island School of Design.

Picture Credits: Library of Congress: Aaron Douglas;
Robert Allen: Alice Walker; Bachrach: Dick Gregory; Mary
Ellen Mark: Maya Angelou; Moorland-Spingarn Research
Center, Howard University: Frederick Douglas, Martin
Luther King, Jr.; Robert Nemiroff: Lorraine Hansberry;
Mario Ruiz: Wallace Terry; Barbra Walz: Bill Cosby

Manufactured in the United States of America
International Standard Book Number: 0-89061-482-2
    6 7 8 9   99 98 97

Readability			
Book One	F–G	Book Three	J–K
Book Two	H–I	Book Four	L–up

Acknowledgments

Acknowledgment is gratefully made to the following publishers and authors for permission to reprint excerpts from these works.

nigger. Text excerpt from *nigger* by Dick Gregory and Robert Lipsyte. Copyright © 1964 by Dick Gregory Enterprises, Inc. Reprinted by permission of E. P. Dutton & Company.

Jubilee. Text excerpt from *Jubilee* by Margaret Walker. Copyright © 1966 by Margaret Walker Alexander. Reprinted by permission of the publisher, Houghton Mifflin Company.

I Know Why the Caged Bird Sings. Text excerpt from *I Know Why the Caged Bird Sings* by Maya Angelou. Copyright © 1969 by Maya Angelou. Reprinted by permission of Random House, Inc.

A View from the Mountaintop, I, II. Reprinted by permission of Joan Daves. Copyright © 1968 by Martin Luther King, Jr. Estate.

Manchild in the Promised Land. Text excerpt from *Manchild in the Promised Land* by Claude Brown. Copyright © 1965 by Claude Brown. Reprinted by permission of The Macmillan Company.

Narrative of the Life of Frederick Douglass. From *The Narrative of the Life of Frederick Douglass.* (1845)

The Boy Who Painted Christ Black. From *American Negro Short Stories*, John Henrik Clarke, Editor. Copyright © 1966 by John Henrik Clarke and published by Hill & Wang. Reprinted with the permission of John Henrik Clarke.

How to Win at Basketball: Cheat. Reprinted by permission of the editors from the January 27, 1970 issue of *Look Magazine.* Copyright © 1970 by Cowles Communications, Inc.

A Raisin in the Sun. From *A Raisin in the Sun* by Lorraine Hansberry. Copyright © 1958 by Lorraine Hansberry. Reprinted by permission of Random House, Inc.

Funeral of a Whale. From *An African Treasury* edited by Langston Hughes. Reprinted by permission of J. Benibengor Blay.

Contents

1 | Introductory Selection

Explains How the Text is Organized and
How to Use It to Maximum Advantage

Vocabulary—The five words below are from the story you are about to read. Study the words and their meanings. Then complete the ten sentences that follow, using one of the five words to fill in the blank in each sentence. Mark your answer by writing the letter of the word on the line before the sentence. Check your answers in the Answer Key on page 106.

A. intent: purpose

B. moderate: calm; avoiding extremes

C. servitude: lack of freedom; slavery

D. corresponding: matching

E. efficient: performing a task easily and skillfully

_____ 1. Some of the selections describe the conditions endured by blacks who lived a life of _____ .

_____ 2. The demands of some black leaders have been extreme; the demands of others have been _____ .

_____ 3. As you work through each selection, you will become more _____ at analyzing written material.

_____ 4. After finishing the book, you will have a good grasp of its _____ .

_____ 5. The skilled reader has learned that each kind of reading matter demands a _____ reading technique.

_____ 6. Some people predicted the book would lead to further separation of the races, but more _____ voices welcomed the book.

_____ 7. In order to be an _____ reader, you must sharpen your critical reading skills.

_____ 8. To communicate with their readers is the _____ of all authors.

_____ 9. Writers, both moderate and extreme, make their arguments in language _____ to their views.

_____ 10. Some of the selections will help you understand the history and background of black people's _____ .

(Before you begin reading this selection, turn to page 8 and record the hours and minutes in the box labeled *Starting Time* at the bottom of the second column. If you are using this text in class and your instructor has made provisions for timing, you need not stop now; read on.)

You are using this text for two purposes: (1) to improve your reading and study skills, (2) to read what black people are saying now and what they have said in the past.

Twenty years ago, when *Selections from the Black* was first published, our nation was just beginning to realize that blacks had a voice and had something to say. Jamestown's intent was to assemble these writings and publish them so that our texts might racially balance the other literature college students were expected to read. When these texts were first published, there were objections from those who felt that a menu of exclusively black writings only served to further isolate blacks from the American mainstream.

Fortunately, moderate thought prevailed, and the concept of a black reading and study skills program was accepted. In the intervening years tens of thousands of students, black and white, have used *Selections from the Black* with satisfaction and success.

In the selections that follow you will read the words of slaves describing their days of oppression. You will read the words of yesterday's leaders—DuBois, Garvey, Washington, and others—and begin to understand the history and background of Negro servitude. You will understand how their thinking influenced their times and ours.

You will read the words of those from the more recent past describing the explosive racial climate of the 1950s and 1960s. This text presents the voices of protest, moderate and defiant, including those silenced by death, exile, and imprisonment. Writers of both extremes are presented here because their words have structured and defined black America.

You will also read the words of people who live under, and struggle against, South Africa's white-minority rule and policy of apartheid. Their messages are important to us because apartheid has become an issue of international proportions.

Black men and women writing about politics, sports, business, journalism, and entertainment have contributed to these selections. Also included are many master writers of fiction; their stories, rich with feeling, are part of the treasury of black literature.

We want you to enjoy these selections, and we want you to learn from them. We especially want you to understand the situation of the black person over time and throughout history.

The other purpose for using this text, that of reading and study improvement, recognizes reality, too: the reality

"It is important to understand the situation of the black person over time and throughout history."

of today. This text will help you to develop skills and techniques necessary for efficiency in our society.

Included in each selection are two Study Skills exercises. In these, you will learn methods of understanding, critical thinking skills, techniques of comprehension, and many other key ways to improve your reading ability. Both Study Skills exercises are designed to assist you in developing efficient reading techniques. As you read the selections in this book, you will find that often one Study Skills exercise leads directly to the next. It is important to read and work the Study Skills exercises consecutively in order to understand fully each subject.

Today's reader must be flexible enough to choose from a supply of skills one that is suitable for each reading task. The skilled reader has learned that each kind of reading matter demands a corresponding reading technique—there is no single "best" way to read. As you complete the selections and exercises in this book, you will find yourself growing in technique.

Using the Text

The twenty selections are designed to be read in numerical order, starting with the Introductory Selection and ending with Selection 20. Because the selections increase in difficulty as you progress through the book, the earlier ones prepare you to handle successfully the upcoming ones.

Here are the procedures to follow for reading each selection.

1. Answer the Vocabulary Questions. Immediately preceding each selection is a vocabulary previewing exercise. The exercise includes five vocabulary words from the selection, their meanings, and ten fill-in-the-blank sentences. To complete each sentence you will fill in the blank with one of the five vocabulary words.

Previewing the vocabulary in such a fashion will give you a head start on understanding the words when you encounter them in the selection. The fill-in-the-blank sentences present each word in context (surrounding words). That provides you with the chance to improve your ability to use context as an aid in understanding words. The efficient use of context is a valuable vocabulary tool.

After you have filled in the blanks in all ten sentences, check your answers in the Answer Key that starts on page 106. Be sure you understand the correct meaning of any wrong answers.

2. Preview before Reading. Previewing acquaints you with the overall content and structure of the selection before you actually read. It is like consulting a road map before taking a trip: planning the route gives you more confidence as you proceed and, perhaps, helps you avoid any unnecessary delays. Previewing should take about a minute or two and is done in this way:

a) Read the Title. Learn the writer's subject and, possibly, his point of view on it.

b) Read the Opening and Closing Paragraphs. These contain the introductory and concluding remarks. Important information is frequently presented in these key paragraphs.

c) Skim through. Try to discover the author's approach to his subject. Does he use many examples? Is his purpose to sell you his ideas? What else can you learn now to help you when you read?

3. Read the Selection. Do not try to race through. Read well and carefully enough so that you can answer the comprehension questions that follow.

Keep track of your reading time by noting when you start and finish. A table on page 110 converts your reading time to a words-per-minute rate. Select the time from the table that is closest to your reading time. Record those figures in the boxes at the end of the selection. There is no one ideal reading speed for everything. The efficient reader varies his speed as the selection requires.

Many selections include a brief biography and perhaps a photograph of the author. Do not include this in your reading time. It is there to introduce you to the writer. Many of the selections have been reprinted from full-length books and novels. Complete information is contained in a bibliography on page 109. If you find a particular selection interesting, you may enjoy reading the entire book.

4. Answer the Comprehension Questions. After you have read the selection, find the comprehension questions that follow. These have been included to test your understanding of what you have read. The questions are diagnostic, too. Because the comprehension skill being measured is identified, you can detect your areas of weakness.

Read each question carefully and, without looking back, select one of the four choices given that answers that question most accurately or most completely. Frequently all four choices, or options, given for a question are *correct*, but one is the *best* answer. For this reason the comprehension questions are highly challenging and require you to be highly discriminating. You may, from time to time, disagree with the choice given in the Answer Key. When this happens, you have an opportunity to sharpen your powers of discrimination. Study the question again and seek to discover why the listed answer may be best. When you disagree with the text, you are thinking; when you objectively analyze and recognize your errors, you are learning.

The Answer Key begins on page 106. Find the answers for your selection and correct your comprehension work. When you discover a wrong answer, circle it and check the correct one.

The boxes following each selection contain space for your comprehension and vocabulary scores. Each correct vocabulary item is worth ten points and each correct comprehension answer is worth ten points.

Pages 111 and 112 contain graphs to be used for plotting your scores and tallying your incorrect responses. On page 111 record your comprehension score at the appropriate intersection of lines, using an X. Use a circle, or some other mark, on the same graph to record your vocabulary results. Some students prefer to use different color inks, or pencil and ink, to distinguish between comprehension and vocabulary plottings.

On page 112 darken in the squares to indicate the comprehension questions you have missed. By referring to the Skills Profile as you progress through the text, you and your instructor will be able to tell which questions give you the most trouble. As soon as you detect a specific weakness in comprehension, consult with your instructor to see what supplementary materials he or she can provide or suggest.

A profitable habit for you to acquire is the practice of analyzing the questions you have answered incorrectly. If time permits, return to the selection to find and underline the passages containing the correct answers. This helps you to see what you missed the first time. Some interpretive and generalization type questions are not answered specifically in the text. In these cases bracket that part of the selection that alludes to the correct answer. Your instructor may recommend that you complete this step outside of class as homework.

5. Complete the Study Skills Exercises. Following the comprehension questions in each chapter is a passage on study skills. Some of the sentences in the passage have blanks where words have been omitted. Next to the passage are groups of five words, one group for each blank. Your task is to complete the passage by selecting the correct word for each of the blanks.

Next are five completion questions to be answered after you have reread the study skills passage.

The same answer key you have been using gives the correct responses for these two study skills exercises.

If class time is at a premium, your instructor may prefer that you complete the exercises out of class.

The following selections in this text are structured just like this introductory one. Having completed this selection and its exercises, you will then be prepared to proceed to Selection 2.

Starting Time		*Finishing Time*	
Reading Time		*Reading Rate*	
Comprehension		*Vocabulary*	

Comprehension— Read the following questions and statements. For each one, put an *x* in the box before the option that contains the most complete or accurate answer. Check your answers in the Answer Key on page 106.

1. How much time should you devote to previewing a selection?
   - ☐ a. Your time will vary with each selection.
   - ☐ b. You should devote about one or two minutes to previewing.
   - ☐ c. No specific time is suggested.
   - ☐ d. None—the instructor times the selection.

2. The way the vocabulary exercises are described suggests that
   - ☐ a. the meaning of a word often depends on how it is used.
   - ☐ b. the final authority for word meaning is the dictionary.
   - ☐ c. words have precise and permanent meanings.
   - ☐ d. certain words are always difficult to understand.

3. The writer of this passage presents the facts in order of
   - ☐ a. importance.
   - ☐ b. purpose.
   - ☐ c. time.
   - ☐ d. operation.

4. *Selections from the Black* is based on which of the following premises?
   - ☐ a. Literature for college students needed to be racially balanced.
   - ☐ b. Black students learn best from black writers.
   - ☐ c. The writings of black authors should provoke student interest.
   - ☐ d. Traditional reading improvement texts are racially unfair.

5. How does the writer feel about reading speed?
   - ☐ a. It is a minimal aspect of the total reading situation.
   - ☐ b. It is second (following comprehension) in the ranking of skills.
   - ☐ c. It is connected to comprehension.
   - ☐ d. It should be developed at an early age.

6. The introductory selection
   - ☐ a. eliminates the need for oral instruction.
   - ☐ b. explains the proper use of the text in detail.
   - ☐ c. permits the student to learn by doing.
   - ☐ d. allows for variety and interest.

7. The introductory selection suggests that
   - ☐ a. most readers are not flexible.
   - ☐ b. students should learn to use different reading skills for different types of reading matter.
   - ☐ c. students today read better than students of the past did.
   - ☐ d. twenty selections is an ideal number for a reading improvement text.

8. The overall tone of this passage is
   - ☐ a. serious.
   - ☐ b. suspenseful.
   - ☐ c. humorous.
   - ☐ d. sarcastic.

9. The author of this selection is probably
   - ☐ a. a doctor.
   - ☐ b. an accountant.
   - ☐ c. an educator.
   - ☐ d. a businessman.

10. The writer of this passage makes his point clear by
   - ☐ a. telling a story.
   - ☐ b. listing historical facts.
   - ☐ c. using metaphors.
   - ☐ d. giving directions.

Comprehension Skills

1. recalling specific facts	6. making a judgment
2. retaining concepts	7. making an inference
3. organizing facts	8. recognizing tone
4. understanding the main idea	9. understanding characters
5. drawing a conclusion	10. appreciation of literary forms

Study Skills, Part One—Following is a passage with blanks where words have been omitted. Next to the passage are groups of five words, one group for each blank. Complete the passage by circling the correct word for each of the blanks.

Previewing

Students frequently ask, "What can I do to improve my reading?" Believe it or not, there is a one-word answer to that ___(1)___ : preview.

(1)   course   question
      statement   theory   lesson

The single most ___(2)___ technique that you can acquire in any reading course is the habit of previewing.

Most students jump in with the first word and try to meet the author's ideas head-on. That is a poor ___(3)___ because it is inefficient.

Athletic coaches, for example, scout their opponents before upcoming games to see how they play. That allows them to form a game ___(4)___ for their team to follow.

To be efficient in reading, you must do the same thing—scout the author to see how he writes. That will help you discover the best way to read the work.

What do you do before assembling a jigsaw puzzle? You probably study the picture to see what the puzzle looks like with the pieces in the proper ___(5)___ .

Do that in reading as well. See the whole picture before you begin putting the words and ideas together. See where the author is going, what he plans to say, and what concepts or examples he uses to present his ideas. If you can discover the author's main point and the arguments ___(6)___ it, you can begin to organize and interpret the ideas right away; hence, you can read intelligently and see how everything fits.

Don't read at a disadvantage. Preview first to get the whole picture. There are no educational guarantees in life, but this is as close as you can come to ensuring better reading and comprehension in less time.

Pregame warmups (to cite another athletic example) improve player performance on the ___(7)___ . Likewise, previewing can improve your performance on the page.

(2)   important   difficult
    statement   divided   natural

(3)   invention   approach
    relationship   value   advantage

(4)   plan   supply
    appearance   overhead   bond

(5)   sources   measures
    places   quantities   perspectives

(6)   supposing   placing
    presenting   discovering   supporting

(7)   whole   field
    rules   trail   water

Study Skills, Part Two—Read the study skills passage again, paying special attention to the lesson being taught. Then, without looking back at the passage, complete each sentence below by writing in the missing word or words. Check the Answer Key on page 106 for the answers to Study Skills, Part One, and Study Skills, Part Two.

1. _____ to improve your performance on the page .

2. Athletic coaches _____ the opponents to see how they play.

3. You should see the whole _____ before you begin putting the words and ideas together.

4. You should look for the concepts or _____ the author uses to present ideas.

5. You can begin to _____ and interpret the author's ideas right from the start.

2 | nigger

by Dick Gregory

Vocabulary—The five words below are from the story you are about to read. Study the words and their meanings. Then complete the ten sentences that follow, using one of the five words to fill in the blank in each sentence. Mark your answer by writing the letter of the word on the line before the sentence. Check your answers in the Answer Key on page 106.

A. hustling: working with great energy

B. catches: attracts, arouses attention

C. credit: time allowed for delayed payment

D. personal: private

E. whip: to lash or beat someone or something

_____ 1. At times, the daily pace made Richard so angry that he wanted to _____ someone.

_____ 2. Momma was happy the electric company had turned on the power, but she knew that their _____ would not last forever.

_____ 3. It was not easy for Richard, working at several different jobs a day and _____ at each.

_____ 4. Richard knew if he angered his mother, she might _____ him.

_____ 5. The wallet was such a special gift; it was his own _____ possession.

_____ 6. As he walks down the street, the bright light of a store display _____ Richard's eye for one solemn moment.

_____ 7. When you are poor, the local grocer won't even let you buy on _____ .

_____ 8. The Christmas carol _____ hold in Richard's mind and resounds long after the music has faded.

_____ 9. It's not easy _____ every day to put bread on the table—some days we go without.

_____ 10. The thoughts Richard shared with his mother about the Almighty were _____ .

It's a sad and beautiful feeling to walk home slow on Christmas Eve after you've been out hustling all day, shining shoes in the white taverns and going to the store for the neighbors and buying and stealing presents from the ten-cent store, and now it's dark and still along the street and your feet feel warm and sweaty

Richard knew whom his mother watched and waited for every Christmas Eve. Richard was waiting for him, too.

inside your tennis sneakers even if the wind finds the holes in your mittens. The electric Santa Clauses wink at you from windows. You stop off at your best friend's house and look at his tree and give him a ball-point pen with his name on it. You reach into your shopping bag and give something to everybody there, even the ones you don't know. It doesn't matter that they don't have anything for you because it feels so good to be in a warm happy place where grownups are laughing. There are Daddies around. Your best friend's so happy and excited, standing there trying on all his new clothes. As you walk down the stairs you hear his mother say: "Boo, you forgot to say good-by to Richard, say good-by to Richard, Boo, and wish him a . . ."

Then you're out on the street again and some of the lights have gone out. You take the long way home, and Mister Ben, the grocer, says: "Merry Christmas, Richard," and you give him a present out of the shopping bag, and you smile at a wino and give him a nickel, and you even wave at Grimes, the mean cop. It's a good feeling. You don't want to get home too fast.

And then you hit North Taylor, your street, and something catches your eye and you lift your head up and it's there in your window. Can't believe it. You start running and the only thing in the whole world you're mad about is that you can't run fast enough. For the first time in a long while the cracked orange door says: "Come on in, little man, you're home now," and there's a wreath and lights in the window and a tree in the kitchen near the coal closet and you hug your Momma, her face hot from the stove. Oh, Momma, I'm so glad you did it like this because ours is new, just for us, everybody else's tree been up all week long for other people to see, and, Momma, ours is up just for us. Momma, oh, Momma, you did it again.

My beautiful Momma smiled at me like Miss America, and my brothers and sisters danced around that little kitchen with the round wooden table and the orange crate chairs.

"Go get the vanilla, Richard," said Momma, "Presley, peel some sweet potatoes. Go get the bread out the oven, Dolores. You get away from that duckling, Garland. Ronald, oh, Ronald, you be good now, stand over there with Pauline. Oh, Richard, my little man, did you see the ham Miz White from the Eat Shop sent by, and the bag of nuts from Mister Myers and the turkey from Miz King, and wouldn't you know, Mister Ben, he . . ."

"Hey, Momma, I know some rich people don't got this much, a ham, and a turkey, Momma. . . ."

"The Lord, He's always looking out for my boys,

Richard, and this ain't all, the white folks'll be by here tomorrow to bring us more things."

Momma was so happy that Christmas, all the food folks brought us and Mister Ben giving us more credit, and Momma even talked the electric man into turning the lights on again.

"Hey, Momma, look here, got a present for Daddy. A cigarette lighter, Momma, there's even a place to scratch a name on it."

"What you scratch on it, Richard, Big Pres or Daddy?"

"Nothing, Momma. Might have to give Daddy's present to old Mister White from the Eat Shop again."

She turned away and when she turned back her eyes were wet. Then she smiled her Miss America smile and grabbed my shoulder. "Richard, my little man, if I show you something, you won't tell nobody, will you?"

"What is it, Momma?"

"I got something for you."

"Oh, Momma, you forgot, everything's under the tree."

"This is something special, just for you, Richard."

"Thanks, Momma, oh, thanks, how'd you know I wanted a wallet, Momma, a real wallet like men have?"

Momma always gave each of us something special like that, something personal that wasn't under the tree, something we weren't supposed to tell the other kids about. It always came out, though. Garland and I'd be fighting and one of us would say, "Momma likes me better than you, look what she gave me," and we both found out the other got a secret present, too.

But I loved that wallet. First thing I did was fill out the address card. If I got hit by a car someone would know who I am. Then I put my dollars in it, just like men do. Ran outside that night and got on a streetcar and pulled out my wallet and handed the conductor a dollar.

"Got anything smaller, boy?"

"Sure, Mister," I said and I pulled out my wallet again and took a dime out of the coin purse and snapped it shut and put the dollar back in the long pocket and closed the wallet and slipped it into my back pocket. Did the same thing on the way back home.

Did we eat that night! It seemed like all the days we went without food, no bread for the baloney and no baloney for the bread, all the times in the summer when there was no sugar for the Kool-Aid and no lemon for the lemonade and no ice at all were wiped away. Man, we're all right.

After dinner I went out the back door and looked at the sky and told God how nobody ever ate like we ate that night, macaroni and cheese and ham and turkey and the old duckling's cooking in the oven for tomorrow. There's even whiskey, Momma said, for people who come by. Thanks, God, Momma's so happy and even the rats and roaches didn't come out tonight and the wind isn't blowing through the cracks.

"How'd you know I wanted a wallet, God?" I wonder if all the rich people who get mink coats and electric trains got that one little thing nobody knew they wanted. You know, God, I'm kinda glad you were born in a manger. I wonder, God, if they had let Mary in the first place she stopped at, would you have remembered tonight? Oh, God, I'm scared. I wish I could die right now with the feeling I have because I know Momma's going to make me mad and I'm going to make her mad, and me and Presley's gonna fight. . . .

"Richard, you get in here and put your coat on. Get in here or I'll whip you."

See what I mean, God, there she goes already and I'm not even cold, I'm all wrapped up in You.

"What's wrong, Richard? Why you look so strange?"

"You wouldn't understand, Momma."

"I would, Richard, you tell me."

"Well, I came out to pray, Momma, way out here so they wouldn't hear me and laugh at me and call me sissy. God's a good God, ain't He, Momma?"

"Yes, Richard."

"Momma, if I tell you something, would you laugh at me, would you say I'm crazy, would you say I was lying? Momma?"

"What is it, Richard?"

"I heard Him talk to me, Momma."

She put her arm around my shoulders and pulled me against her. "He talks to people, Richard, some people that are real special and good like you. Do me a favor, Richard?"

"Sure, Momma."

"Next time you talk to Him, ask Him to send Daddy home."

"Let me stay up and look out the window with you, Momma."

"Everybody's in bed, Richard."

"All my life, Momma, I wanted to stay up with you on Christmas Eve and look out that window with you, Momma. I won't laugh at you."

Dick Gregory first gained fame as a stand-up comedian, beginning his career in Chicago nightclubs in 1958. He became active in the civil rights movement in the 1960s, and in 1968 ran for president of the United States as the Peace and Freedom Party candidate. In the late 1960s and early 1970s he was an outspoken critic of American policy in Vietnam. On the subject of conflict between his entertainment career and his political activities, Gregory says: "Active involvement in the struggle for human dignity is the real value in life. A career is secondary." Gregory was the recipient of the Ebony-Topaz Heritage and Freedom award in 1978.

"What you mean, Richard?"

"You're waiting on him, ain't you? I know, Momma, every Christmas Eve you take a bath and put on that perfume and those clothes from the rich white folks and get down there on your knees in front of that window looking for Daddy."

"Richard, you better get on to bed."

"I know, Momma, that whiskey ain't for people coming by, that's for Daddy."

"Richard, you go on to bed and when he gets here I'll wake you up."

"No, Momma, I want to sit up with you . . . Momma?"

"Yes, Richard?"

"I shoulda got a present for Mister White, 'cause I know Daddy's coming to get his this year."

Starting Time		Finishing Time	
Reading Time		Reading Rate	
Comprehension		Vocabulary	

Comprehension— Read the following questions and statements. For each one, put an *x* in the box before the option that contains the most complete or accurate answer. Check your answers in the Answer Key on page 106.

1. Boo is Richard's
   □ a. best friend.
   □ b. older brother.
   □ c. younger brother.
   □ d. neighbor.

2. Apparently, Richard's family is
   □ a. rich.
   □ b. crazy.
   □ c. poor.
   □ d. uncaring.

3. The writer of this story relates the events in
  - □ a. sequential order.
  - □ c. historical order.
  - □ b. order of importance.
  - □ d. spatial order.

4. Which of the following best gives the main thought of the passage?
  - □ a. angry and mean
  - □ c. hated by all
  - □ b. poor, but proud
  - □ d. crazy about life

5. The reader's first clue that Richard's father does not live at home comes when Richard says
  - □ a. "You're waiting on him, ain't you?"
  - □ b. "Might have to give Daddy's present to old Mister White from the Eat Shop again."
  - □ c. "I know Daddy's coming to get his this year."
  - □ d. "There are Daddies around."

6. For the purposes of the story, Richard's father is
  - □ a. a dream come true.
  - □ b. an alcoholic.
  - □ c. a criminal.
  - □ d. a "Santa Claus" image.

7. Richard felt at ease praying to the Almighty because he
  - □ a. went to church often.
  - □ b. needed someone to turn to.
  - □ c. felt the Christmas spirit and knew it was a good time to pray.
  - □ d. was able to identify with the Christ of the manger.

8. As Richard walks home his mood changes from near depression to
  - □ a. guilt.
  - □ b. apathy.
  - □ c. humor.
  - □ d. excitement.

9. The Christmas season intensifies Momma's desire to
  - □ a. prepare special meals.
  - □ b. get her husband back.
  - □ c. keep her family together.
  - □ d. buy special gifts.

10. This selection is
  - □ a. a fable.
  - □ b. a folktale.
  - □ c. an autobiography.
  - □ d. a biography.

Comprehension Skills	
1. recalling specific facts	*6. making a judgment*
2. retaining concepts	*7. making an inference*
3. organizing facts	*8. recognizing tone*
4. understanding the main idea	*9. understanding characters*
5. drawing a conclusion	*10. appreciation of literary forms*

Study Skills, Part One—Following is a passage with blanks where words have been omitted. Next to the passage are groups of five words, one group for each blank. Complete the passage by circling the correct word for each of the blanks.

How to Preview, I

Previewing is known by many names. It is called *surveying* and *prereading* too. The first three steps in previewing are as follows:

1. Read the Title. You would normally do that before reading a selection, but in previewing we want you to be _(1)_ of what you can *learn* from the title. Not only can you learn the author's subject, you can frequently learn how he or she *feels* about that subject. W.H. Auden once wrote an essay entitled *Poetry Must Praise.* From the title you can discern the author's feeling, and you would expect to read _(2)_ supporting his position and illustrations demonstrating his case. With just that little bit of _(3)_, a reader can approach the selection intelligently, knowing what to expect.

An author named Mark Clifton wrote an article called *The Dread Tomato Addiction.* Judging by the title, you

(1)   hopeful   aware
  jealous   indifferent   certain

(2)   articles   announcements
  letters   arguments   references

(3)   information   courage
  direction   hesitancy   informality

could reasonably expect to find ___(4)___ or satire in the author's account.

Headlines and titles are thought to be quite influential by authors and editors. Indeed, many magazines survive on the appeal or ___(5)___ value of the titles of their articles.

2. Read the Subheads. In textbooks especially, and in many magazines as well, subheads follow the title to give the reader more information on the subject. In textbooks, subheads often take the form of one-line digests of the chapter—"Here's what we are going to cover." In magazines, "teaser" statements follow the title to further spark the reader's ___(6)___ . Look for subheads whenever you are previewing.

3. Read the Illustrations. If a picture or illustration accompanies the article, don't glance at it and move on, *read* it. Interpret it to learn what you can about the ___(7)___ of the article. You have no doubt heard it said that a picture is worth a thousand words. You can prove the worth of that observation by studying the illustrations when previewing. In other words, see what you can learn visually before reading.

(4)   imagination   intelligence
         humility   tragedy   humor

(5)   sensitive   shock
         serious   survival   literary

(6)   currency   urgency
         satisfaction   disgust   interest

(7)   flavor   attitude
         content   author   popularity

Study Skills, Part Two—Read the study skills passage again, paying special attention to the lesson being taught. Then, without looking back at the passage, complete each sentence below by writing in the missing word or words. Check the Answer Key on page 106 for the answers to the Study Skills, Part One, and Study Skills, Part Two.

1. The first step in previewing is _____ .

2. The first step can tell you not only the author's subject, but also his

   _____ about the subject.

3. Many magazines survive on the appeal of the _____ of their

   articles.

4. The subheads in textbooks frequently give a one-line _____

   of the chapters.

5. The Chinese have said that a picture is worth a thousand _____ .

3 | **Jubilee**

by Margaret Walker

Vocabulary—The five words below are from the story you are about to read. Study the words and their meanings. Then complete the ten sentences that follow, using one of the five words to fill in the blank in each sentence. Mark your answer by writing the letter of the word on the line before the sentence. Check your answers in the Answer Key on page 106.

A. compassion: mercy, kindness

B. justify: to defend an action

C. parched: dried from heat or fever

D. brutalized: savagely beaten or abused

E. vague: unclear, hazy, or confused

_____ 1. As Vyry regained consciousness she did not recognize her own children, and her memory of Marse John was _____ .

_____ 2. The salt stung the wounds on Vyry's back, and fever _____ her lips and eyes.

_____ 3. Vyry knew she walked toward her punishment, realizing with each step that Grimes and his men would show no _____ .

_____ 4. As Vyry began to black out from the pain, the lights became dim and _____ .

_____ 5. After the first lash, Vyry knew for sure that she was going to be terribly _____ .

_____ 6. Caline and May Liza had enough _____ to care for Vyry.

_____ 7. It was easy for Grimes's men to _____ beating a runaway slave.

_____ 8. Soon the _____ skin around the mouth began to swell and crack.

_____ 9. The once _____ skin now began to heal in a loose flap over one breast.

_____ 10. When Marse John returned, Big Missy would be asked to _____ the beating.

That morning going back to the plantation everything around her seemed unreal. The fog lifted slowly and through the misty morning she moved steadily toward what she knew would be her punishment. The children were not alarmed, and for that she was glad. Little Jim trotted homeward without a whimper while the baby sleeping in her arms was soundless. Grimes and his men did not speak to her but she knew that they were ruthless and there would be no compassion. It was a well-known fact that if a slave ran away and was caught in the act, flogging was the punishment. She could expect a whipping. She did not let herself think ahead beyond each step. Once she thought about Marse John. Perhaps he would interfere and not let them beat her. But she knew this was not possible because he was never at home whenever anything happened. He had been gone three days and might be gone two or three more; supposedly, he had gone to town on business. Maybe they can put it off until he comes home. No, she also knew better than that. Big Missy would want to get this over with before Marster's return. It was always easier for Missy Salina to explain things later and justify them most after they had occurred. Vyry was not at all surprised, therefore, when Grimes took her children from her on entering Marster's back yard. He led her to the whipping post not far from the wet fields where the field hands were not working this morning because the ground was too wet.

Two of Grimes's men tied her hands together as if she were folding them to pray, and then stretched them high above her head. They tied her to the post so that her feet were tied together and crossed above the ground. It seemed as if she were hanging on the post in mid-air, her feet stretched as far as they could stretch without touching the earth beneath her and her hands stretched as far above her head without reaching beyond the post. Her body was naked to the waist, and she braced herself to bear the lash of the whip upon her naked flesh.

Grimes did not choose to beat her. One of the guards who was generally hired to whip slaves was now ready to flog Vyry.

He took the whip in his hands. It was a raw-hide coach-whip used to spur the horses. He twirled it up high over his head, and when he came down with it he wrapped it all the way around her body and cut neatly into her breast and across her back all at the same time with one motion while the whip was a-singing in the air. It cut the air and her flesh and cried "zing" and Vyry saw stars that were red and black and silver, and there were a thousand of those stars in the midnight sky and her head felt as if it would split open and the whip cut her like a red-hot poke iron or a knife that was razor sharp and cut both ways. The whip burned like fire and cut the blood out of her and stung like red-hot pins

Vyry feared that her tormentors had left her to die at the whipping post. Surely another slave would rescue her soon—or did they think she was already dead?

sticking in her flesh while her head was reeling and whirling. It hurt so badly she felt as if her flesh were a single molten flame, and before she could catch her breath and brace herself again, he had wrapped the whip around her the second time. When she heard the whip go "zing" the second time and felt the stars rocking in her head, she opened her mouth to scream, but her throat was too dry to holler and she gritted her teeth and smashed her head hard against the post in order to steel herself once more to bear the pain. When he wrapped her all around with the whip the third time she thought she heard a roaring noise like thunder rumbling and a forest of trees falling in a flood. Everything went black; she was caught up in the blackness of a storm. She was whirling around in a cutting, fiery-wind while the fire was burning her flesh like a tormenting fever and she kept sinking down in the fire and fighting the blackness until every light went out like a candle and she fainted.

She never did know how many lashes he gave her, whether he cut her the required seventy-five times as he was told to do, or whether he quit short of that number, thinking she was already dead and further beating was useless.

When she came to she heard a buzzing in her ears and everything still looked black though it wasn't yet evening. It must have been afternoon but there was no sunlight. Somebody had cut her loose from the post and left her huddled in a heap on the ground at the bottom of the whipping post. At first she thought it was night because all she could see looked black. She looked at her hands and her arms and she pulled at the shreds of rags on her legs and all her flesh looked black. She was as black as a man's hat and she was black like that all over. She looked around her on the ground and saw blood spattered and clotted around her while something glistened white like salt. Although her mind was still dazed she knew now why her back was still on fire and she felt as if she were lying on a bed of red-hot needles and iron. It was the salt somebody had thrown on her bleeding raw back. She was too weak to move. She wondered why she was still living, because they must have meant to kill her. "Why has God let me live?" *All the black people must be scared to come and get me till it is black dark. Maybe they think I'm dead. Lawd, have mercy, Jesus! Send somebody to get me soon, please Jesus!* The flies were making the buzzing sound and she felt her body throbbing in a rhythm with the flies. Fever parched her lips and eyes and her bruised hands and ran through her brutalized flesh.

After dark the other house servants came and got her and took her to her cabin. Caline and May Liza poured warm oil on her back and washed it free of salt. Then they put her on a soft pallet of rags and let her sleep.

When the fever had parched its course through Vyry and the raw bruises began to form healing scars, the cloud in her mind began to lift. She could remember deep waves and complete inundation in the dark waters that threatened to take her under. She could not remember her own children and when they were brought to her she did not know them. Once she thought she saw Marse John standing over her and thought she heard him cursing terrible oaths, but even his face was vague in her memory. Caline and May Liza brought her hot broth to drink and coaxed her to swallow but she did not know them either or remember what they had done. After three days the fever seemed to be leaving her and her mind began to clear. She was too weak to speak above a whisper, and when she was able to examine herself she saw where one of the lashes had left a loose flap of flesh over her breast like a tuck in a dress. It healed that way.

Margaret Walker studied at Northwestern University, majoring in English, and received her M.A. in 1940 from the University of Iowa. In 1942, Walker's book *For My People* was published as selection of the year in the Yale University Series of Younger Poets. She was awarded a fellowship at the University of Iowa in 1963, where she received a Ph.D. and completed her novel *Jubilee*.

Walker taught English at Livingstone College and West Virginia State College and has been a member of the faculty at Jackson State University in Mississippi since 1949.

Starting Time		*Finishing Time*	
Reading Time		*Reading Rate*	
Comprehension		*Vocabulary*	

Comprehension — Read the following questions and statements. For each one, put an *x* in the box before the option that contains the most complete or accurate answer. Check your answers in the Answer Key on page 106.

1. Vyry's fever lasted
   □ a. two days.
   □ b. three days.
   □ c. six days.
   □ d. a week.

2. Vyry's friends waited until after dark to help her because they
   □ a. were superstitious.
   □ b. thought she was dead.
   □ c. feared for their safety.
   □ d. were indifferent.

3. The details in this story are given in
   □ a. a simple list.
   □ b. the order in which they happened.
   □ c. order of importance.
   □ d. ascending order.

4. What is the main thought of this story?
   □ a. If runaway slaves were caught, they were flogged.
   □ b. White masters treated their black slaves with respect.
   □ c. Caline and May poured warm oil on Vyry's wounds.
   □ d. Vyry was a good slave even though she tried to run away.

5. The beating was
   □ a. incompetent.
   □ b. professional.
   □ c. resisted.
   □ d. unnecessary.

6. Marse John is to Big Missy as
   □ a. kindness is to cruelty.
   □ b. fear is to prejudice.
   □ c. business is to pleasure.
   □ d. opportunity is to action.

7. Marse John's angry curses in reaction to Vyry's beating were directed at
   □ a. Vyry.
   □ b. Big Missy and Grimes.
   □ c. all the slaves.
   □ d. Caline and May Liza.

8. The author portrays Vyry's feelings and reactions during the whipping
   □ a. intensely.
   □ b. superficially.
   □ c. fiendishly.
   □ d. objectively.

9. The personality of Grimes and his men is
mostly revealed through their
☐ a. appearance. ☐ c. dialogue.
☐ b. actions. ☐ d. thoughts.

10. Considering the tone of the selection,
its title is
☐ a. sad. ☐ c. ironic.
☐ b. justified. ☐ d. appropriate.

Study Skills, Part One—Following is a passage with blanks where words have been omitted. Next to the passage are groups of five words, one group for each blank. Complete the passage by circling the correct word for each of the blanks.

How to Preview, II

We have seen how previewing is necessary for intelligent reading. The first three steps, as you have read, are (1) read the title, (2) read the subheads, and (3) read the illustrations. Here are the last three steps:

4. Read the Opening Paragraph. The first paragraph is the author's opening, his first opportunity to address the __(1)__ . This paragraph is also called the introductory paragraph because it is precisely that—an introduction to the article or chapter. Opening paragraphs are __(2)__ with different purposes in mind. Some authors announce what they plan to say in the main body of the work. Other authors tell us why they are writing the article or chapter and why it is important for us to read it. Still other authors will do what speakers do—start with a story or anecdote to __(3)__ the stage. That provides the setting or mood they need to present their material.

5. Read the Closing Paragraph. The next step in previewing is to go to the __(4)__ and read the last paragraph. That is the author's last chance to address the reader. If he has any closing remarks or final thoughts, or if he wishes to reemphasize or restate principal thoughts or arguments, he will do it in the closing paragraph. Since it is the closing paragraph, it must express concluding or summarizing thoughts. You'll see what the __(5)__ considers important in his closing paragraph.

6. Skim Through. Finally, before completing your preview, quickly skim the article or chapter to see what else you can __(6)__ . Watch for headings and numbers that indicate important __(7)__ of the author's presentation. You may, for example, learn that the material is divided into four or five major aspects; that knowledge will be helpful when you are reading.

(1)   envelope   reader
     crowd   audience   package

(2)   written   found
     analyzed   used   developed

(3)   set   light
     fill   fix   decorate

(4)   book   middle
     beginning   end   library

(5)   reader   teacher
     author   editor   student

(6)   understand   skim
     learn   teach   know

(7)   additions   reversals
     proofs   introductions   facets

Study Skills, Part Two—Read the study skills passage again, paying special attention to the lesson being taught. Then, without looking back at the passage, complete each sentence below by writing in the missing word or words. Check the Answer Key on page 106 for the answers to Study Skills, Part One, and Study Skills, Part Two.

1. The first paragraph is usually an _____ to the article.

2. Authors use the first paragraph to announce their plans, to give their reason for writing the article, or to provide a _____ .

3. In the concluding paragraph, the author may restate _____ points.

4. In the concluding paragraph, the author may gather the facts in the article, and _____ them.

5. Finally, we should quickly _____ the article one more time to complete the preview.

4 | I Know Why the Caged Bird Sings

by Maya Angelou

Vocabulary—The five words below are from the story you are about to read. Study the words and their meanings. Then complete the ten sentences that follow, using one of the five words to fill in the blank in each sentence. Mark your answer by writing the letter of the word on the line before the sentence. Check your answers in the Answer Key on page 106.

A. exactness: accuracy or precision

B. perpetually: never stopping; permanently

C. fumed: fretted and stormed in anger

D. construed: analyzed or understood

E. dilemma: a problem situation calling for a decision

_____ 1. Looking at the green glass coffee cups, Margaret immediately saw the answer to her _____ .

_____ 2. Everything in the house had its own special place, and the _____ of that arrangement was a source of discomfort at first.

_____ 3. Margaret became so upset by the name change that she _____ all the way from the porch to the kitchen.

_____ 4. Mrs. Cullinan's many errands kept Margaret _____ busy.

_____ 5. Margaret was upset by the name change even though Glory explained that she had _____ Mrs. Cullinan's actions in the wrong way.

_____ 6. After a week of learning the routine, the _____ of it was still tiring.

_____ 7. If Mrs. Cullinan thought that Margaret dropped the dishes on purpose, she probably _____ the situation correctly.

_____ 8. Margaret's _____ was that she wanted to quit but didn't have a good reason to do so.

_____ 9. The woman, holding a piece of broken plate in her hand, _____ at the young girl.

_____ 10. Miss Glory's role in life was to _____ wait on her mistress.

During my tenth year, a white woman's kitchen became my finishing school.

Mrs. Viola Cullinan was a plump woman who lived in a three-bedroom house somewhere behind the post office. She was singularly unattractive until she smiled, and then the lines around her eyes and mouth which made her look perpetually dirty disappeared, and her face looked like the mask of an impish elf. She usually rested her smile until late afternoon when her women friends dropped in and Miss Glory, the cook, served them cold drinks on the closed-in porch.

The exactness of her house was inhuman. This glass went here and only here. That cup had its place and it was an act of impudent rebellion to place it anywhere else. At twelve o'clock the table was set. At 12:15 Mrs. Cullinan sat down to dinner (whether her husband had arrived or not). At 12:16 Miss Glory brought out the food.

It took me a week to learn the difference between a salad plate, a bread plate and a dessert plate.

Mrs. Cullinan kept up the tradition of her wealthy parents. She was from Virginia. Miss Glory, who was a descendant of slaves that had worked for the Cullinans, told me her history. She had married beneath her (according to Miss Glory). Her husband's family hadn't had their money very long and what they had "didn't 'mount to much."

As ugly as she was, I thought privately, she was lucky to get a husband above or beneath her station. But Miss Glory wouldn't let me say a thing against her mistress. She was very patient with me, however, over the housework. She explained the dishware, silverware and servants' bells.

The large round bowl in which soup was served wasn't a soup bowl, it was a tureen. There were goblets, sherbet glasses, ice-cream glasses, wine glasses, green glass coffee cups with matching saucers, and water glasses. I had a glass to drink from, and it sat with Miss Glory's on a separate shelf from the others. Soup spoons, gravy boat, butter knives, salad forks and carving platter were additions to my vocabulary and in fact almost represented a new language. I was fascinated with the novelty, with the fluttering Mrs. Cullinan and her Alice-in-Wonderland house.

Her husband remains, in my memory, undefined. I lumped him with all the other white men that I had ever seen and tried not to see.

On our way home one evening, Miss Glory told me that Mrs. Cullinan couldn't have children. She said that she was too delicate-boned. It was hard to imagine bones at all under those layers of fat. Miss Glory went on to say that the doctor had taken out all her lady organs. I reasoned that a pig's organs included the lungs, heart and liver, so if Mrs. Cullinan was walking around without those essentials, it explained why she drank alcohol out of unmarked bottles. She was keeping herself embalmed.

Mrs. Cullinan tried to take away Margaret's symbol of herself—her name. Was it worth losing her job over? Margaret thought so.

When I spoke to my brother Bailey about it, he agreed that I was right, but he also informed me that Mr. Cullinan had two daughters by a colored lady and that I knew them very well. He added that the girls were the spitting image of their father. I was unable to remember what he looked like, although I had just left him a few hours before, but I thought of the Coleman girls. They were very light-skinned and certainly didn't look very much like their mother (no one ever mentioned Mr. Coleman).

My pity for Mrs. Cullinan preceded me the next morning like the Cheshire cat's smile. Those girls, who could have been her daughters, were beautiful. They didn't have to straighten their hair. Even when they were caught in the rain, their braids still hung down straight like tamed snakes. Their mouths were pouty little cupid's bows. Mrs. Cullinan didn't know what she missed. Or maybe she did. Poor Mrs. Cullinan.

For weeks after, I arrived early, left late and tried very hard to make up for her barrenness. If she had had her own children, she wouldn't have had to ask me to run a thousand errands from her back door to the back door of her friends. Poor old Mrs. Cullinan.

Then one evening Miss Glory told me to serve the ladies on the porch. After I set the tray down and turned toward the kitchen, one of the women asked, "What's your name, girl?" It was the speckled-faced one. Mrs. Cullinan said, "She doesn't talk much. Her name's Margaret."

"Is she dumb?"

"No. As I understand it, she can talk when she wants to but she's usually quiet as a little mouse. Aren't you, Margaret?"

I smiled at her. Poor thing. No organs and couldn't even pronounce my name correctly.

"She's a sweet little thing, though."

"Well, that may be, but the name's too long. I'd never bother myself. I'd call her Mary if I was you."

I fumed into the kitchen. That horrible woman would never have the chance to call me Mary because if I was starving I'd never work for her. I decided I wouldn't pee on her if her heart was on fire. Giggles drifted in off the porch and into Miss Glory's pots. I wondered what they could be laughing about.

Whitefolks were so strange. Could they be talking about me? Everybody knew that they stuck together better than the Negroes did. It was possible that Mrs. Cullinan had friends in St. Louis who heard about a girl from Stamps being in court and wrote to tell her. Maybe she knew about Mr. Freeman.

My lunch was in my mouth a second time and I went outside and relieved myself on the bed of four-o'clocks. Miss Glory thought I might be coming down with something and told me to go on home, that Momma would give me some herb tea, and she'd explain to her mistress.

I realized how foolish I was being before I reached the pond. Of course Mrs. Cullinan didn't know. Otherwise she wouldn't have given me the two nice dresses that Momma cut down, and she certainly wouldn't have called me a "sweet little thing." My stomach felt fine, and I didn't mention anything to Momma.

That evening I decided to write a poem on being white, fat, old and without children. It was going to be a tragic ballad. I would have to watch her carefully to capture the essence of her loneliness and pain.

The very next day, she called me by the wrong name. Miss Glory and I were washing up the lunch dishes when Mrs. Cullinan came to the doorway. "Mary?"

Miss Glory asked, "Who?"

Mrs. Cullinan, sagging a little, knew and I knew. "I want Mary to go down to Mrs. Randall's and take her some soup. She's not been feeling well for a few days."

Miss Glory's face was a wonder to see. "You mean Margaret, ma'am. Her name's Margaret."

"That's too long. She's Mary from now on. Heat that soup from last night and put it in the china tureen and, Mary, I want you to carry it carefully."

Every person I knew had a hellish horror of being "called out of his name." It was a dangerous practice to call a Negro anything that could be loosely construed as insulting because of the centuries of their having been called niggers, jigs, dinges, blackbirds, crows, boots and spooks.

Miss Glory had a fleeting second of feeling sorry for me. Then as she handed me the hot tureen she said, "Don't mind, don't pay that no mind. Sticks and stones may break your bones, but words . . . You know, I been working for her for twenty years."

She held the back door open for me. "Twenty years. I wasn't much older than you. My name used to be Hallelujah. That's what Ma named me, but my mistress give me 'Glory,' and it stuck. I likes it better too."

I was in the little path that ran behind the houses when Miss Glory shouted, "It's shorter too."

For a few seconds it was a tossup over whether I would laugh (imagine being named Hallelujah) or cry (imagine letting some white woman rename you for her convenience). My anger saved me from either outburst. I had to quit the job, but the problem was going to be how to do it. Momma wouldn't allow me to quit for just any reason.

"She's a peach. That woman is a real peach." Mrs. Randall's maid was talking as she took the soup from me, and I wondered what her name used to be and what she answered to now.

For a week I looked into Mrs. Cullinan's face as she called me Mary. She ignored my coming late and leaving early. Miss Glory was a little annoyed because I had begun to leave egg yolk on the dishes and wasn't putting much heart in polishing the silver. I hoped that she would complain to our boss, but she didn't.

Then Bailey solved my dilemma. He had me describe the contents of the cupboard and the particular plates she liked best. Her favorite piece was a casserole shaped like

Aside from being a well-known writer, Maya Angelou has worked as an actress, film director, lecturer, and musician. During the 1960s, she worked as an editor and reporter in Africa, becoming the first woman editor of an English-language magazine. She published several novels in the 1970s and wrote the screenplay and musical score for the film *Georgia, Georgia* in 1972. In 1975 she received the *Ladies Home Journal* "Woman of the Year Award" for Communications. Other honors include a Tony nomination for best supporting actress for her performance in the 1977 television series *Roots,* numerous honorary degrees, and a place in the Black Filmmakers Hall of Fame.

Maya Angelou is currently a member of Actor's Equity, the Director's Guild of America, and the advisory board of the Women's Prison Association.

a fish and the green glass coffee cups. I kept his instructions in mind, so on the next day when Miss Glory was hanging out clothes and I had again been told to serve the old biddies on the porch, I dropped the empty serving tray. When I heard Mrs. Cullinan scream, "Mary!" I picked up the casserole and two of the green glass cups in readiness. As she rounded the kitchen door I let them fall on the tiled floor.

I could never absolutely describe to Bailey what happened next, because each time I got to the part where she fell on the floor and screwed up her ugly face to cry, we burst out laughing. She actually wobbled around on the floor and picked up shards of the cups and cried, "Oh, Momma. Oh, dear Gawd. It's Momma's china from Virginia. Oh, Momma, I'm sorry."

Miss Glory came running in from the yard and the women from the porch crowded around. Miss Glory was almost as broken up as her mistress. "You mean to say she broke our Virginia dishes? What we gone do?"

Mrs. Cullinan cried louder, "That clumsy nigger. Clumsy little black nigger."

Old speckled-face leaned down and asked, "Who did it, Viola? Was it Mary? Who did it?"

Everything was happening so fast I can't remember whether her action preceded her words, but I know that Mrs. Cullinan said, "Her name's Margaret, goddamn it, her name's Margaret!" And she threw a wedge of the broken plate at me. It could have been the hysteria which put her aim off, but the flying crockery caught Miss Glory right over her ear and she started screaming.

I left the front door wide open so all the neighbors could hear.

Mrs. Cullinan was right about one thing. My name wasn't Mary.

Starting Time		Finishing Time	
Reading Time		Reading Rate	
Comprehension		Vocabulary	

Comprehension— Read the following questions and statements. For each one, put an *x* in the box before the option that contains the most complete or accurate answer. Check your answers in the Answer Key on page 106.

1. Margaret managed to lose her job by following the advice of
   ☐ a. Mrs. Cullinan.　　☐ c. Mr. Cullinan.
   ☐ b. Miss Glory.　　　☐ d. Bailey.

2. Margaret's attitude during her stay in Mrs. Cullinan's house ranged from
   ☐ a. submission to fear to anger.
   ☐ b. fascination to protest to revolt.
   ☐ c. pleasure to suspicion to confusion.
   ☐ d. resentment to tolerance to acceptance.

3. The events in the story begin
   ☐ a. before Margaret is born.
   ☐ b. when Margaret is ten years old.
   ☐ c. after Margaret is married.
   ☐ d. after Margaret dies.

4. Which of the following best expresses the main idea of the selection?
   ☐ a. To thine own self be true.
   ☐ b. What's in a name?
   ☐ c. This was the most unkind cut of all.
   ☐ d. A rose by any other name would smell as sweet.

5. We can conclude from this story that Mrs. Cullinan was
   ☐ a. undernourished.　☐ c. depressed.
   ☐ b. not poor.　　　　☐ d. unwed.

6. To Margaret, the lifestyle Mrs. Cullinan and her friends enjoyed seemed
   ☐ a. futile.　　　　☐ c. fascinating.
   ☐ b. productive.　　☐ d. depressing.

7. By the end of the story, Margaret's pity for Mrs. Cullinan
   ☐ a. was gone.　　☐ c. was forgotten.
   ☐ b. had deepened.　☐ d. was unchanged.

8. The two elements that best describe the tone of the selection are
   ☐ a. generosity and concern.
   ☐ b. fear and sarcasm.
   ☐ c. amusement and understanding.
   ☐ d. irony and humor.

9. The statement "She usually rested her smile until late afternoon when her women friends dropped in" tells us that Mrs. Cullinan was
   ☐ a. usually carefree.
   ☐ b. humorous.
   ☐ c. not always cheerful.
   ☐ d. generous to a fault.

10. The description "their braids still hung down straight like tamed snakes" shows the use of
    ☐ a. an opinion.
    ☐ b. a comparison.
    ☐ c. a contrast.
    ☐ d. an exaggeration.

Comprehension Skills	
1. recalling specific facts	6. making a judgment
2. retaining concepts	7. making an inference
3. organizing facts	8. recognizing tone
4. understanding the main idea	9. understanding characters
5. drawing a conclusion	10. appreciation of literary forms

Study Skills, Part One—Following is a passage with blanks where words have been omitted. Next to the passage are groups of five words, one group for each blank. Complete the passage by selecting the correct word for each of the blanks.

Question the Author

You've probably heard it said that you'll never learn if you don't ask questions.

Why is an inquisitiveness associated with learning? We speak of the student seeking knowledge, or of the ___(1)___ mind, and both of those concepts imply asking or questioning.

(1)　　restless　　　　inactive
　　　trained　　inquiring　　satisfied

That is because learning is not a passive process; it is something we *do*. Learning is a(n) ___(2)___ . We must go after it and seek it out. That is why we say that questioning is part of learning.

Good students question the author following previewing by asking, "What can I expect to learn from this chapter or article? Based on my ___(3)___ what are some of the topics likely to be presented? What will the author tell me about this subject?" Questions of that nature frame the subject and provide an ___(4)___ to be filled in when reading.

Another thing we hope to discover from questioning is the author's method of presentation. There are many methods an author can use in presenting material. Some may ask questions and answer them, using that ___(5)___ to make the subject easier to learn. Some may give details, or describe and illustrate. Others still may compare and contrast. Whatever the method, discover it and put it to use when studying.

In many books the questions are there waiting to be used. Check your textbooks. Are there questions following the chapters? If so, use them during previewing to instill the inquisitiveness so necessary to learning. Those are special questions—they tell us what important points the author really ___(6)___ you to learn in each chapter.

Develop the technique of questioning. Try whenever you study to ___(7)___ questions you expect to find answered.

(2)   activity   avocation
       possession   vacation   accident

(3)   education   prereading
       attitude   condition   skills

(4)   summary   introduction
       reason   lecture   outline

(5)   material   technique
       position   career   review

(6)   discovers   avoids
       forces   expects   forbids

(7)   create   remember
       enjoy   distrust   encourage

Study Skills, Part Two—Read the study skills passage again, paying special attention to the lesson being taught. Then, without looking back at the passage, complete each sentence below by writing in the missing word or words. Check the Answer Key on page 106 for the answers to Study Skills, Part One, and Study Skills, Part Two.

1. In order to learn, it is necessary to _____ .

2. Ask yourself what you expect to _____ from the article.

3. One of your aims should be to discover the author's method of

   _____ .

4. One method the author may use is comparison and _____ .

5. Be sure to check for questions _____ the chapters.

A View from the Mountaintop, I

by Martin Luther King, Jr.

Vocabulary—The five words below are from the story you are about to read. Study the words and their meanings. Then complete the ten sentences that follow, using one of the five words to fill in the blank in each sentence. Mark your answer by writing the letter of the word on the line before the sentence. Check your answers in the Answer Key on page 106.

A. trek: a long journey

B. eternal: unending and everlasting

C. vacillating: hesitating in making a decision, wavering

D. grappling: struggling, as in wrestling with a problem

E. agenda: items of concern listed in some type of order

_____ 1. When God's people left Egypt, they began a _____ toward the Promised Land.

_____ 2. The masses of people are rising up and _____ with the issue of freedom.

_____ 3. Dr. King was a decisive man not known for _____ when making choices.

_____ 4. In Dr. King's view, many of the issues discussed by the ancient Greeks were great and _____ .

_____ 5. We have to stand firm and be resolved, for there is no strength in _____ minds.

_____ 6. Fair treatment for all people should be the first item on everyone's _____ .

_____ 7. One of the strengths of America is the _____ right to protest for fair and equal treatment.

_____ 8. There are people on this earth _____ with hunger and poverty.

_____ 9. We do have a complete _____ that could be followed.

_____ 10. Black people have come a long way over the years, but the _____ has not been, nor will it be, an easy one.

If I were standing at the beginning of time with the pulse of energy ticking, a kind of general with a panoramic view of the whole of human history up to now, and the Almighty said to me, "Martin Luther King, which age would you like to live in?" I would take my mental flight by Egypt. And I would watch God's children in their magnificent trek from the dark dungeons of Egypt; across the Red Sea; through the wilderness; on toward the Promised Land, and in spite of its magnificence, I wouldn't stop there.

I would move on by Greece and take my mind to Mount Olympus. I would see Plato, Aristotle, Socrates, Euripides and Aristophanes, assembled around the Parthenon. And I would watch them around the Parthenon as they discuss the great and eternal issues of reality, but I wouldn't stop there.

I would go on even to the great heyday of the Roman Empire. And I would see developments through various emperors and leaders. But I wouldn't stop there.

I would even come up to the day of the Renaissance, and get a good picture of all that the Renaissance did for the cultural and aesthetic life of man, but I wouldn't stop there. I would even go by the way that the man for whom I am named had his habitat. And I would watch Martin Luther as he tacks his 95 theses on the door of the church of Wittenberg. But I wouldn't stop there.

I would come on up even to 1863 and watch the vacillating President by the name of Abraham Lincoln finally come to the conclusion that he had to sign the Emancipation Proclamation. But I wouldn't stop there.

I would even come up to the early thirties, and see a man grappling with the problems of the bankruptcy of this nation. And come with an eloquent cry that we have "nothing to fear but fear itself." But I wouldn't stop there.

Strangely enough, I would turn to the Almighty and say, "If you allow me to live just a few years in the second half of the twentieth century, I will be happy." Now that's a strange statement to make because the world is all messed up, the nation is sick, trouble is in the land, confusion all around . . . that's a strange statement. But I know somehow that only when it is dark enough can you see the stars. And I see God working in this period of the twentieth century in a way that men in some strange way are responding. Something is happening in our world. The masses of people are rising up, whether they are in Johannesburg, South Africa, Nairobi, Kenya, Ghana, New York City, Atlanta, Georgia, Jackson, Mississippi, or Memphis, Tennessee, the cry is always the same: "We want to be free."

I'm happy to live in this period in which we're going to have to grapple with the problems that men have been trying to grapple with through history but the demand didn't force them to do it. Survival demands that we

In Dr. King's last message before his murder, he calls on his people to work together in the cause of freedom and for the betterment of black society.

grapple with them. Men for years now have been talking about war and peace. But now, no longer can they just talk about it. It is no longer a choice between violence and nonviolence in this world. It's nonviolence or nonexistence. That is where we are today.

Now, I'm just happy that God has allowed me to live in this period, to see what is unfolding. And I'm happy that He's allowed me to be in Memphis. I can remember when Negroes were just going around, as Ralph [Abernathy] has said so often, "scratchin' heavy to the ditch and laughin' when they were not tearful." But that day is all over. We mean business now and we are determined to gain our rightful place in God's world.

And that's all this whole thing is about; we aren't engaged in any negative protest and in any negative arguments with anybody. We are saying that we are determined to be men, we are determined to be people. We are saying that we are God's children, and if we are God's children, we are going to have to live like we are supposed to live. Now what does all this mean in this great period of history? It means that we've got to stay together and maintain unity.

You know, whenever Pharaoh wanted to prolong the period of slavery in Egypt, he had a favorite formula for doing it. What was that? He kept the slaves fighting among themselves. But whenever the slaves get together, something happens in Pharaoh's court, and he cannot hold the slaves in slavery; when the slaves get together, that's the beginning of getting out of slavery. Now let us maintain unity.

We've got to go on in Memphis just like that. I call upon you to be with us when we go out Monday. We'll have an injunction and we'll go on into court tomorrow morning to fight this illegal, unconstitutional injunction. All we say to "massa" is "be true to what you said on paper." If I lived in China, or even Russia, or in any totalitarian country, maybe I could understand some of these illegal injunctions. Maybe I could understand the denial of certain basic First Amendment privileges, because they have committed themselves to that over there. But somewhere I read of the freedom of assembly; somewhere I read of the freedom of speech, somewhere I read of the freedom of press, somewhere I read that the greatness of America is the right to protest for right.

What is beautiful to me is to see all these ministers of the Gospel here tonight. And I want you to thank them. Because so often preachers aren't concerned about anything but themselves. And I'm always happy to see a relevant minister. It's all right to talk about long white robes over yonder in all of its symbolism. But all too many people need some suits and dresses and shoes to wear down here. It's all right to talk about streets flowing with milk and honey. But God has commanded us to be concerned about the slums down here and the children who can't eat three square meals a day. It's all right to talk about the New Jerusalem, but one day God's creatures must talk about the new New York, the new Atlanta, the new Philadelphia, the new Los Angeles, the new Memphis, Tennessee.

This is what we have to do. Always anchor our external direction with the power of economic control. Now we're poor people. Individually, we're poor, when you compare us with white society in America. We're poor. But collectively, that means all of us together, collectively we are richer than most of the nations in the world. Did you ever think about that?

After you leave the United States, Soviet Russia, Great Britain, West Germany, France, I could name others, the American Negro collectively is richer than most nations in the world. We have an annual income of more than 30 billion dollars a year, which is more than all of the exports of the United States and more than the national budget of Canada. Did you know that?

That's power right there if we know how to pool it. We don't have to argue with anybody. We don't need any bricks and bottles; we don't need any molotov cocktails. We just need to go around to these stores and massive industries in our country and say, "God sent us by here, to say to you that you're not treating His children right. And we come by here to ask you to make the first item on your agenda fair treatment where God's children are concerned. Now if you are not prepared to do that, we do have an agenda that we must follow. And our agenda calls for withdrawing economic support from you." Up to now, only the garbage men have been feeling pain. Now we must kind of redistribute the pain.

Now let me say as I move to my conclusion, that we've got to give ourselves to this struggle until the end. Nothing will be more tragic than to stop at this point in Memphis. We've got to see it through. When we go on our march, you need to be there. If it means leaving work, if it means leaving school, be there! Be concerned about your brother. You may not be on strike, but either we go up together or we go down together.

Martin Luther King, Jr., a Baptist minister, was the main leader of the American civil rights movement in the 1950s and '60s. An advocate of peaceful change, he led many nonviolent civil rights demonstrations and was the catalyst in gaining support for desegregation in the South. In 1957, Dr. King helped create the Southern Christian Leadership Conference. In 1964, he was awarded the Nobel Peace Prize for his efforts to create awareness of social injustice.

King graduated from Morehouse College in Atlanta in 1948, received a divinity degree from Crozer Theological Seminary in Chester, Pennsylvania, and received a Ph.D. in theology from Boston University in 1955. After serving as pastor of the Dexter Avenue Baptist Church in Montgomery, Alabama, he joined his father in 1960 as co-pastor of the Ebenezer Baptist Church in Atlanta, Georgia.

Despite his advocacy of nonviolence, Dr. King was often the target of threats and attacks. In 1968, while in Memphis, Tennessee, to support a strike by black garbage men, King was assassinated.

In the United States, Dr. King's birthday is observed as a national holiday on the third Monday in January.

Starting Time			Finishing Time	
Reading Time			Reading Rate	
Comprehension			Vocabulary	

Comprehension— Read the following questions and statements. For each one, put an *x* in the box before the option that contains the most complete or accurate answer. Check your answers in the Answer Key on page 106.

1. According to Dr. King, black Americans must awaken to their
   - ☐ a. economic power.
   - ☐ b. black power.
   - ☐ c. numerical power.
   - ☐ d. academic power.

2. The selection ends with an appeal to
   - ☐ a. unity and commitment.
   - ☐ b. humility and reason.
   - ☐ c. emotion and piety.
   - ☐ d. fortitude and determination.

3. The first part of this selection is arranged in
   - ☐ a. order of significance.
   - ☐ b. numerical order.
   - ☐ c. chronological order.
   - ☐ d. spatial order.

4. Which of the following best summarizes the appeal made in the selection?
   - ☐ a. Tomorrow Will Be Too Late
   - ☐ b. Freedom Through Unity
   - ☐ c. In God We Trust
   - ☐ d. Black Is Beautiful

5. Dr. King points out most of the nations in the world are
   ☐ a. poorer than black Americans collectively.
   ☐ b. not economically united.
   ☐ c. constantly in a state of unrest.
   ☐ d. made up of a nonwhite populace.

6. According to King, many of the preachers of today
   ☐ a. preach violent protest.
   ☐ b. are self-ordained ministers.
   ☐ c. are concerned with black poverty.
   ☐ d. refuse to deal with reality.

7. In mentioning some things that black people "don't need," King implies that black people are trying to solve their problems by using
   ☐ a. economic pressure.   ☐ c. violence.
   ☐ b. religion.   ☐ d. abject poverty.

8. In the last paragraph of the selection King sounds
   ☐ a. determined.   ☐ c. peaceful.
   ☐ b. humorous.   ☐ d. apathetic.

9. Which of the following best describes Martin Luther King, Jr.?
   ☐ a. passive
   ☐ b. nonviolent
   ☐ c. stubborn
   ☐ d. aggressive

10. King's "But I wouldn't stop there" is an example of his use of
   ☐ a. an exclamation.
   ☐ b. comparisons.
   ☐ c. repetition.
   ☐ d. cause and effect.

Comprehension Skills

1. recalling specific facts	6. making a judgment
2. retaining concepts	7. making an inference
3. organizing facts	8. recognizing tone
4. understanding the main idea	9. understanding characters
5. drawing a conclusion	10. appreciation of literary forms

Study Skills, Part One—Following is a passage with blanks where words have been omitted. Next to the passage are groups of five words, one group for each blank. Complete the passage by circling the correct word for each of the blanks.

How to Concentrate, I

If you have trouble concentrating, consider yourself normal. That is the universal student complaint. And it is not restricted just to students. Everyone at some __(1)__ finds it hard to concentrate.

Concentrating means giving all of your attention to the issue at hand. The trouble comes from distractions, the inability to shut out __(2)__ matters and noises.

Are there ways to improve your ability to concentrate? Yes.

1. Increase Motivation. You've no doubt observed that you concentrate more easily on matters about which you are highly motivated. Motivation is one key to concentration. You don't become distracted when you're __(3)__ interested in something.

Those matters that have some immediate and specific goal motivate people most. We study intently our local *Driver's Manual* when the goal of getting a driver's license is at hand. The goal of passing tomorrow's __(4)__ often helps students concentrate quite effectively the night before.

Your task in increasing motivation, then, is to set a goal that means enough to help you develop the kind of concentration you need. Even a short-range goal might be __(5)__ to give you the motivation you need at the moment.

(1)   school   time
    step   position   goal

(2)   harmful   important
    interfering   enjoyable   distant

(3)   falsely   really
    not   somewhat   partially

(4)   time   burden
    plan   place   quiz

(5)   enough   lacking
    harmful   excessive   accepted

2. Prepare to Study. As simple as that may sound, it ___(6)___ . Prepare yourself properly and completely for the task of studying. Distractions will of course be a bother if you don't arrange to remove them, or to remove yourself from them. No one can concentrate in a busy, noisy room. Try to find a quiet, well-lighted spot equipped with a table and a chair. Seated at the table, upright in the chair, you will be in the ___(7)___ posture for studying and concentrating.

(6)   shows   fails
       simplifies   works   hurts

(7)   moderate   worst
       best   only   second

Study Skills, Part Two—Read the study skills passage again, paying special attention to the lesson being taught. Then, without looking back at the passage, complete each sentence below by writing in the missing word or words. Check the Answer Key on page 106 for the answers to Study Skills, Part One, and Study Skills, Part Two.

1. Students are not the only people who have _____ concentrating.

2. Concentrating means giving your exclusive _____, shutting out everything else.

3. _____ is one key to concentration. We don't become distracted when we're interested.

4. It's easy to concentrate on something when you have a definite _____ in mind.

5. When you prepare to study, find a comfortable, quiet place, free from _____ .

6 # A View from the Mountaintop, II

by Martin Luther King, Jr.

Vocabulary—The five words below are from the story you are about to read. Study the words and their meanings. Then complete the ten sentences that follow, using one of the five words to fill in the blank in each sentence. Mark your answer by writing the letter of the word on the line before the sentence. Check your answers in the Answer Key on page 106.

A. meandering: following a winding, wandering course

B. conducive: promoting or helping bring about a result

C. lure: to attract for the purpose of snaring

D. seizure: the act of taking something by force

E. concerned: worried, anxious

_____ 1. At this point in his life, Dr. King was no longer _____ about longevity.

_____ 2. On the road to Jericho there were many places to which a robber could _____ a passerby in order to rob him.

_____ 3. Every American should be _____ with the plight of black people in America.

_____ 4. A situation in which all citizens have certain rights is _____ to change.

_____ 5. The road from Jerusalem was a winding, _____ road.

_____ 6. In Christ's time, people who traveled the road to Jericho risked _____ by robbers.

_____ 7. A person should not _____ others into doing things against their better judgment.

_____ 8. Dr. King did not preach violence and _____; his message was one of peaceful unity.

_____ 9. In writing his speech, Dr. King organized his _____ thoughts into a powerfully directed address.

_____ 10. America's democratic system is _____ to the attaining of individual rights.

I remember when Mrs. King and I were first in Jerusalem. We rented a car to go from Jerusalem down to Jericho. And as soon as we got on that road, I said to my wife, "I can see why Jesus used this as the setting for the parable of the Good Samaritan." It's a winding, meandering road. It's really conducive for ambushing. You start out in Jerusalem which is about 1200 feet above sea level. And by the time you get down to Jericho, 15 or 20 minutes later, you're about 2200 feet below sea level. That's a dangerous road. In the days of Jesus it came to be known as the Bloody Pass.

And you know it's possible that the priest and the Levite looked over that man on the ground and wondered if the robbers were still around. It's possible that they felt the man on the ground was merely faking—acting like he had been robbed and beaten in order to lure them there for quick and easy seizure. And so the first question that the priest asked, the first question that the Levite asked was, "If I stop to help this man, what will happen to me?" But then the Good Samaritan came by. And he reversed the question. "If I do not stop to help this man, what will happen to him?" That's the question before you tonight. Not if I stop to help the sanitation workers what will happen to my job; not if I stop to help the sanitation workers what will happen to all of the hours that I usually spend in my office every day of every week as a pastor. The question is not if I stop to help this man in need, what will happen to me. The question is, if I do *not* stop to help the sanitation workers, what will happen to them. That's the question.

Let us rise up tonight with a greater readiness. Let us stand with a greater determination. And let us move on, in these powerful days, these days of challenge, to make America what it ought to be. We have an opportunity to make America a better nation. And I want to praise God once more for allowing me to be here with you.

You know, several years ago I was in New York City, autographing the first book that I had written. While sitting autographing books, a demented woman came up. The only question I heard from her was, "Are you Martin Luther King?" And I was looking down writing. I said "yes." The next minute I felt something beating on my chest. Before I knew it, I had been stabbed by this demented woman. I was rushed to Harlem Hospital. It was a dark Saturday afternoon. X-rays revealed that the tip of the blade was on the edge of my aorta, the main artery. And once that's punctured, you drown in your own blood. That's the end of you. It came out in the *New York Times* the next morning that if I would have merely sneezed, I would have died.

Well, about four days later, they allowed me to read some of the mail that came in from all over the United States and the world. Kind letters came in. I read a few, but one of them I will never forget. I had received one

Dr. King continues his final message, in which he urges black people to meet the challenge of making a better America.

from the President and the Vice President: I've forgotten what those telegrams said. I had received a visit and a letter from the Governor of New York, but I've forgotten what that letter said. But there was another letter. It came from a young girl. I looked at that letter, and I'll never forget it. It said simply: "Dear Dr. King, I am a 9th grade student at the White Plains High School."

She said, "While it should not matter I'd like to mention that I'm a white girl. I read in the paper of your misfortune and of your suffering. And I read that if you had sneezed, you would have died. I'm simply writing you to say that I'm so happy that you didn't sneeze."

And I want to say tonight that I, too, am happy that I didn't sneeze. Because if I had sneezed, I wouldn't have been around here till 1960 when students all over the South started sitting in at lunch counters. And I knew that if they were sitting in, they were really standing up for the best in the American dream, and taking the whole nation back to those great wells of democracy which were dug deep by the founding fathers in the Declaration of Independence and the Constitution. If I had sneezed, I wouldn't have been down here in 1961 when we decided to take a ride for freedom and ended segregation in interstate travel. If I had sneezed, I wouldn't have been around here in 1962 when Negroes in Albany, Georgia, decided to straighten their backs up. And whenever men and women straighten their backs up, they are going somewhere; because a man can't ride your back unless it is bent. If I had sneezed, I wouldn't have been here in 1963; black people down in Birmingham, Alabama, aroused the conscience of this nation and brought into being the Civil Rights bill. If I had sneezed, I wouldn't have had a chance later that year to try to tell America about a tune that I had heard. If I had sneezed, I wouldn't have been down in Selma, Alabama, to start a movement there. If I had sneezed, I wouldn't have been in Memphis to see a community rally around those brothers and sisters who were suffering. I'm so happy that I didn't sneeze.

It really doesn't matter what happens now. I left Atlanta this morning, and as we got started on the plane, there was trouble. The pilot said, over the public address system, "We're sorry for the delay. But we have Dr. Martin Luther King on the plane and to be sure that all of the bags were checked and to be sure that nothing would be wrong on the plane, we had to check out everything carefully and we've had the plane protected and guarded all night." Then I got into Memphis and some began to say the threats or talk about the threats that were out, and what would happen to me from some of our sick white brothers.

Well, I don't know what will happen now. We've got some difficult days ahead, but it really doesn't matter with me now because I've been to the mountaintop. And

I don't mind. Like anybody, I would like to live a long life. Longevity has its place. But I'm not concerned about that now. I just want to do God's will. And He has allowed me to go up to the mountain. And I've looked over, and I've seen the Promised Land. I may not get there with you, but I want you to know tonight that we as a people will get to the Promised Land. So I'm happy tonight. I'm not worried about anything. I'm not fearing any man. Mine eyes have seen the glory of the coming of the Lord.

Martin Luther King, Jr.'s civil rights activities began in 1955 in Montgomery, Alabama, where he led a boycott of the city's segregated bus system. As a result of the boycott, the United States Supreme Court ordered Montgomery to provide integrated seating on public buses.

As the civil rights movement grew, King was involved in major demonstrations in Albany, Georgia, and Birmingham, Alabama. His most famous appearance was at the massive ''March on Washington'' in 1963. Over 200,000 Americans, black and white, gathered at the Lincoln Memorial in Washington, D.C. There King delivered his well-known ''I Have a Dream'' speech.

Since his death in 1968, King's wife, Coretta Scott King, has continued to pursue the goals of the civil rights movement. She has won numerous awards for her work advocating peace, women's rights, and nonviolent social change.

Starting Time		*Finishing Time*	
Reading Time		*Reading Rate*	
Comprehension		*Vocabulary*	

Comprehension— Read the following questions and statements. For each one, put an *x* in the box before the option that contains the most complete or accurate answer. Check your answers in the Answer Key on page 106.

1. In the days of Jesus, the road from Jerusalem to Jericho was known as
   - ☐ a. Holy Way.
   - ☐ b. God's Highway.
   - ☐ c. the Sacred Ground.
   - ☐ d. the Bloody Pass.

2. Dr. King attributes his attack in New York City to
   - ☐ a. overwork.
   - ☐ b. his attacker's mental illness.
   - ☐ c. propaganda published by white racists.
   - ☐ d. his book.

3. Dr. King describes the journey from Jerusalem to Jericho using
   - ☐ a. spatial relationships.
   - ☐ b. a simple list.
   - ☐ c. details given in order of importance.
   - ☐ d. chronological order.

4. What is the main question Dr. King wants people to ask themselves after hearing the parable of the Good Samaritan?
   - ☐ a. If I do not stop to help this man, what will happen to me?
   - ☐ b. Who is going to help the sanitation workers?
   - ☐ c. If I do not stop to help the workers, what will happen to them?
   - ☐ d. Why should I stop to help the workers?

5. The plane delay leads us to believe that Dr. King's dream
   - ☐ a. was opposed by some people.
   - ☐ b. could never be realized.
   - ☐ c. met with disapproval from the pilot and crew.
   - ☐ d. would become a dream shared by all.

6. The element that made the young girl's letter memorable was its
   - ☐ a. white author.
   - ☐ b. expression of concern.
   - ☐ c. honest innocence.
   - ☐ d. surprising humor.

7. Dr. King's speech was delivered in support of
   - ☐ a. law and order.
   - ☐ b. a new book.
   - ☐ c. free enterprise.
   - ☐ d. striking workers.

8. The tone of the selection is one of
   - ☐ a. undisguised irony.
   - ☐ b. simple humor.
   - ☐ c. fervent optimism.
   - ☐ d. blatant criticism.

9. In the Memphis speech, Dr. King is revealed as being
   ☐ a. an activist.   ☐ c. political.
   ☐ b. inflammatory.   ☐ d. a racist.

10. When Dr. King says the students were "taking the whole nation back to those great wells of democracy which were dug deep by the founding fathers," he is using
   ☐ a. a metaphor.   ☐ c. onomatopoeia.
   ☐ b. a simile.   ☐ d. personification.

Comprehension Skills

1. recalling specific facts
2. retaining concepts
3. organizing facts
4. understanding the main idea
5. drawing a conclusion
6. making a judgment
7. making an inference
8. recognizing tone
9. understanding characters
10. appreciation of literary forms

Study Skills, Part One—Following is a passage with blanks where words have been omitted. Next to the passage are groups of five words, one group for each blank. Complete the passage by circling the correct word for each of the blanks.

How to Concentrate, II

We've seen two techniques that we can use to improve concentration. They involve (1) increasing motivation, and (2) preparing to study. Here are three other techniques:

3. Set a Time. Have you ever noticed how timing brings out peak efficiency? Almost every athletic event is closely timed; or else the participants are competing against time. For instance, in track events the winner's time generates as much interest as does the place in which she ___(1)___ . Timing is a natural incentive to competitive athletes— they can't resist the ___(2)___ . You can make use of your sense of competition when you have an assignment to complete or a lesson to study. Set a time for the completion of the task. Your inclination to beat the ___(3)___ may inspire the sustained concentration you need. Timing, put simply, builds concentration.

4. Pace the Assignment. Trying to do too much too soon will destroy concentration, not increase it. We know that we cannot sustain full concentration for very long ___(4)___ , especially when we're not in the habit. When an assignment is long, involved and complex, it's best not to try to ___(5)___ it at one sitting. Segment the task into twenty-minute parcels and spread out the periods of study. Returning to an ___(6)___ task makes it easier to regain concentration, because we want to see the job completed. That desire to get the job done helps build the kind of concentration we need.

5. Organize the Task. One major reason students can't concentrate is that their assignment is unplanned and vague. When that is the case, the assignment itself is a distraction. Through the skills of Previewing and Questioning you should be able to organize the assignment into a series of ___(7)___ and specific tasks. List exactly what you wish to learn or accomplish in the designated periods of study. Then set up a time framework and stick to it.

(1)   finishes   stumbles
        begins   races   lives

(2)   challenge   warmup
        glory   event   injury

(3)   others   system
        enemy   clock   competition

(4)   periods   confinements
        sessions   attempts   skills

(5)   understand   delay
        complete   sustain   ignore

(6)   overlooked   agreeable
        understood   unfinished   optimistic

(7)   related   ordinary
        assigned   difficult   remembered

Study Skills, Part Two—Read the study skills passage again, paying special attention to the lesson being taught. Then, without looking back at the passage, complete each sentence below by writing in the missing word or words. Check the Answer Key on page 106 for the answers to Study Skills, Part One, and Study Skills, Part Two.

1. To help concentration, it is suggested that you set a _____ for completion of the assignment.

2. It is natural to try and complete the task in a _____ period of time than was suggested.

3. If an assignment is very long, divide it into sections, and _____ out the periods of study.

4. It is important to organize the assignment into several definite _____.

5. Before you begin, _____ what you want to accomplish in the following period of study.

7 | Manchild in the Promised Land

by Claude Brown

Vocabulary—The five words below are from the story you are about to read. Study the words and their meanings. Then complete the ten sentences that follow, using one of the five words to fill in the blank in each sentence. Mark your answer by writing the letter of the word on the line before the sentence. Check your answers in the Answer Key on page 107.

A. regularly: on a regular basis

B. engaged: involved in an activity

C. measures: steps taken as a means to an end

D. plight: a predicament or problem situation

E. prophecies: predictions about the future

_____ 1. Mama would take away my clothes and shoes; even so my _____ was not serious.

_____ 2. Dad, taking serious _____, beat me each time I played hookey.

_____ 3. Attending school _____ was not as much fun as playing the game of hookey.

_____ 4. We _____ in the daily activities of stealing and sneaking around the neighborhood.

_____ 5. When the yellow card came in the mail, I knew my _____ had worsened.

_____ 6. Dad took to beating me _____.

_____ 7. At that time, Buddy was _____ in a rock throwing contest.

_____ 8. All the _____ about my future were dark and gloomy.

_____ 9. The people at the Children's Centers did not use strict _____ for punishing runaways.

_____ 10. People in the area began to make _____ about my chances for leading a productive life.

I remembered sitting on the stoop with Danny, years before, when a girl came up and started yelling at him. She said that her mother didn't want her brother to hang out with Danny any more, because Danny had taught her brother how to play hookey. When the girl had gone down the street, I asked Danny what hookey was. He said it was a game he would teach me as soon as I started going to school.

Danny was a man of his word. He was my next-door neighbor, and he rang my doorbell about 7:30 A.M. on the second day of school. Mama thanked him for volunteering to take me to school. Danny said he would have taught me to play hookey the day before, but he knew that Mama would have to take me to school on the first day. As we headed toward the backyard to hide our books, Danny began to explain the great game of hookey. It sounded like lots of fun to me. Instead of going to school, we would go all over the city stealing, sneak into a movie, or go up on a roof and throw bottles down into the street. Danny suggested that we start the day off by waiting for Mr. Gordon to put out his vegetables; we could steal some sweet potatoes and cook them in the backyard. I was sorry I hadn't started school sooner, because hookey sure was a lot of fun.

Before I began going to school, I was always in the streets with Danny, Kid, and Butch. Sometimes, without saying a word, they would all start to run like hell, and a white man was always chasing them. One morning as I entered the backyard where all the hookey players went to draw up an activity schedule for the day, Butch told me that Danny and Kid had been caught by Mr. Sands the day before. He went on to warn me about Mr. Sands, saying Mr. Sands was that white man who was always chasing somebody and that I should try to remember what he looked like and always be on the lookout for him. He also warned me not to try to outrun Mr. Sands, "because that cat is fast." Butch said, "When you see him, head for a backyard or a roof. He won't follow you there."

During the next three months, I stayed out of school twenty-one days. Dad was beating the hell out of me for playing hookey, and it was no fun being in the street in the winter, so I started going to school regularly. But when spring rolled around, hookey became my favorite game again. Mr. Sands was known to many parents in the neighborhood as the truant officer. He never caught me in the street, but he came by my house many mornings to escort me to class. This was one way of getting me to school, but he never found a way to keep me there. The moment my teacher took her eyes off me, I was back on the street. Every time Dad got a card from Mr. Sands, I got bruises and welts from Dad. The beatings had only a temporary effect on me. Each time, the beatings got worse; and each time, I promised never to

As a young boy, Claude was unofficially voted least likely to live to the age of twenty-one.

play hookey again. One time I kept that promise for three whole weeks.

The older guys had been doing something called "catting" for years. That catting was staying away from home all night was all I knew about the term. Every time I asked one of the fellows to teach me how to cat, I was told I wasn't old enough.

As time went on, I learned that guys catted when they were afraid to go home and that they slept everywhere but in comfortable places. The usual places for catting were subway trains, cellars, unlocked cars, under a friend's bed, and in vacant newsstands.

One afternoon when I was eight years old, I came home after a busy day of running from the police, truant officer, and storekeepers. The first thing I did was to look in the mailbox. This had become a habit with me even though I couldn't read. I was looking for a card, a yellow card. That yellow card meant that I would walk into the house and Dad would be waiting for me with his razor strop. He would usually be eating and would pause just long enough to say to me, "Nigger, you got a whippin' comin'." My sisters, Carole and Margie, would cry almost as much as I would while Dad was beating me, but this never stopped him. After each beating I got, Carole, who was two years older than I, would beg me to stop playing hookey. There were a few times when I thought I would stop just to keep her and Margie, my younger sister, from crying so much. I decided to threaten Carole and Margie instead, but this didn't help. I continued to play hookey, and they continued to cry on the days that the yellow card got home before I did.

Generally, I would break open the mailbox, take out the card, and throw it away. Whenever I did this, I'd have to break open two or three other mailboxes and throw away the contents, just to make it look good.

This particular afternoon, I saw a yellow card, but I couldn't find anything to break into the box with. Having some matches in my pockets, I decided to burn the card in the box and not bother to break the box open. After I had used all the matches, the card was not completely burned. I stood there getting more frightened by the moment. In a little while, Dad would be coming home; and when he looked in the mailbox, anywhere would be safer than home for me.

This was going to be my first try at catting out. I went looking for somebody to cat with me. My crime partner, Buddy, whom I had played hookey with that day, was busily engaged in a friendly rock fight when I found him in Colonial Park. When I suggested that we go up on the hill and steal some newspapers, Buddy lost interest in the rock fight.

We stole papers from newsstands and sold them on the subway trains until nearly 1 A.M. That was when the third cop woke us and put us off the train with the usual threat. They would always promise to beat us over the head with a billy and lock us up. Looking back, I think the cops took their own threats more seriously than we did. The third cop put us off the Independent Subway at Fifty-ninth Street and Columbus Circle. I wasn't afraid of the cops, but I didn't go back into the subway—the next cop might have taken me home.

In 1945, there was an Automat where we came out of the subway. About five slices of pie later, Buddy and I left the Automat in search of a place to stay the night. In the center of the Circle, there were some old lifeboats that the Navy had put on display.

Buddy and I slept in the boat for two nights. On the third day, Buddy was caught ringing a cash register in a five-and-dime store. He was sent to Children's Center, and I spent the third night in the boat alone. On the fourth night, I met a duty-conscious cop, who took me home. That ended my first catting adventure.

Dad beat me for three consecutive days for telling what he called "that dumb damn lie about sleeping in a boat on Fifty-ninth Street." On the fourth day, I think he went to check my story out for himself. Anyhow, the beatings stopped for a while, and he never mentioned the boat again.

Before long, I was catting regularly, staying away from home for weeks at a time. Sometimes the cops would pick me up and take me to a Children's Center. The Centers were located all over the city. At some time in my childhood, I must have spent at least one night in all of them except the one on Staten Island.

The procedure was that a policeman would take me to the Center in the borough where he had picked me up. The Center would assign someone to see that I got a bath and was put to bed. The following day, my parents would be notified as to where I was and asked to come and claim me. Dad was always in favor of leaving me where I was and saying good riddance. But Mama always made the trip. Although Mama never failed to come for me, she seldom found me there when she arrived. I had no trouble getting out of Children's Centers, so I seldom stayed for more than a couple of days.

When I was finally brought home—sometimes after weeks of catting—Mama would hide my clothes or my shoes. This would mean that I couldn't get out of the house if I should take a notion to do so. Anyway, that's how Mama had it figured. The truth of the matter is that these measures only made getting out of the house more difficult for me. I would have to wait until one of the fellows came around to see me. After hearing my plight, he would go out and round up some of the gang, and they would steal some clothes and shoes for me. When they had the clothes and shoes, one of them would come to the house and let me know. About ten minutes later, I would put on my sister's dress, climb down the back fire escape, and meet the gang with the clothes.

If something was too small or too large, I would go and steal the right size. This could only be done if the item that didn't fit was not the shoes. If the shoes were too small or large I would have trouble running in them and probably get caught. So I would wait around in the backyard while someone stole me a pair.

Mama soon realized that hiding my clothes would not keep me in the house. The next thing she tried was threatening to send me away until I was twenty-one. This was only frightening to me at the moment of hearing it. Ever so often, either Dad or Mama would sit down and have a heart-to-heart talk with me. These talks were very moving. I always promised to mend my bad ways. I was always sincere and usually kept the promise for about a week. During these weeks, I went to school every day and kept my stealing at a minimum. By the beginning of the second week, I had reverted back to my wicked ways, and Mama would have to start praying all over again.

The neighborhood prophets began making prophecies about my life-span. They all had me dead, buried, and forgotten before my twenty-first birthday. These predictions were based on false tales of policemen shooting at me, on truthful tales of my falling off a trolley car into the midst of oncoming automobile traffic while hitching a ride, and also on my uncontrollable urge to steal. There was much justification for these prophecies. By the time I was nine years old, I had been hit by a bus, thrown into the Harlem River (intentionally), hit by a car, severely beaten with a chain. And I had set the house afire.

While Dad was still trying to beat me into a permanent conversion, Mama was certain that somebody had worked roots on me. She was writing to all her relatives in the South for solutions, but they were only able to say, "that boy musta been born with the devil in him." Some of them advised Mama to send me down there, because New York was no place to raise a child. Dad thought this was a good idea, and he tried to sell it to Mama. But Mama wasn't about to split up her family. She said I would stay in New York, devil or no devil. So I stayed in New York, enjoying every crazy minute.

Born in 1937 in New York City, Claude Brown spent his early life as a member of a street gang known as the Harlem Buccaneers. He also worked as a confidence man, drug dealer, and jazz pianist.
In 1965, Brown received a B.A. from Howard University. Brown has been the recipient of a Metropolitan Community Methodist Church grant, and, for furthering intergroup relations, the Saturday Review Ansfield-Wolf Award. He resides in New York City.

Starting Time		Finishing Time	
Reading Time		Reading Rate	
Comprehension		Vocabulary	

Comprehension — Read the following questions and statements. For each one, put an *x* in the box before the option that contains the most complete or accurate answer. Check your answers in the Answer Key on page 107.

1. The boys catted when they
   □ a. had just played hookey.
   □ b. were planning a robbery.
   □ c. burned the mail.
   □ d. were afraid to go home.

2. Some of Mama's relatives suggested that
   □ a. she change her son's environment.
   □ b. Dad beat the devil out of his son.
   □ c. a spell had been cast on her son.
   □ d. she leave her son at a Center.

3. When the author played hookey, his father beat him. Their actions demonstrate what kind of relationship?
   □ a. comparison and contrast
   □ b. opinion versus fact
   □ c. cause and effect
   □ d. a time-order relationship

4. The main point of the story is that
   □ a. the author was a streetwise kid with a future that looked dim.
   □ b. hookey was a fun game to play with friends.
   □ c. the writer was a good student and friend who was led astray by the wrong element.
   □ d. all black kids belong to ghetto gangs.

5. As opposed to Dad, Mama handled their son with
   □ a. patience.
   □ b. severity.
   □ c. psychology.
   □ d. trust.

6. The conditions that produced the situation described in this selection were
   □ a. religious and educational.
   □ b. political and educational.
   □ c. economic and religious.
   □ d. economic and social.

7. The author hadn't learned to read because
   □ a. he lacked interest.
   □ b. he had poor teachers.
   □ c. there were no books at home.
   □ d. he was too young.

8. Despite all the troubles the author describes, the tone of the selection is often
   □ a. remorseful.   □ c. light and funny.
   □ b. bitter.   □ d. full of whimsy.

9. As a young boy, the author was
   □ a. hopeless and corrupt.
   □ b. torn between home and street influences.
   □ c. sad and lonely.
   □ d. torn between school and gang influences.

10. The selection is
   □ a. autobiographical.   □ c. descriptive.
   □ b. biographical.   □ d. narrative.

Comprehension Skills	
1. recalling specific facts	*6. making a judgment*
2. retaining concepts	*7. making an inference*
3. organizing facts	*8. recognizing tone*
4. understanding the main idea	*9. understanding characters*
5. drawing a conclusion	*10. appreciation of literary forms*

Study Skills, Part One —Following is a passage with blanks where words have been omitted. Next to the passage are groups of five words, one group for each blank. Complete the passage by circling the correct word for each of the blanks.

How to Remember

Just as there are ways to help build concentration, there are techniques we can __(1)__ to help us remember what we study. Here are three of those techniques:

1. Plan to Remember. That is so obvious that we tend to overlook its value, but it works. Tell yourself that you want to remember something and you will. For example,

(1)   create   adjust
     forget   employ   discard

if you are like most people, you have trouble recalling the name of someone you have just met. The next time you're ___(2)___ , plan to remember the person's name. Say to yourself, "I'll listen carefully. I'll repeat the name to be sure I have it. I *will* remember it." You'll find there's nothing to it; you'll probably remember that name for the rest of your life.

Many of us complain that we have short memories, but the truth is we simply don't try to or plan to remember— we don't program our memories. From now on, make up your mind before you read or study that you ___(3)___ to, and will, remember.

2. Review the Material. Most forgetting occurs shortly after the learning has been done. More new material crowds out what information we've just studied, and we have trouble recalling that information. The problem of too much information can be overcome by reviewing. A review, by definition, is not a total rereading of the ___(4)___ assignment. In fact, the technique of previewing, which you have previously learned, is actually reviewing in advance; hence, you already know what reviewing is and how to do it. Previewing again and recalling your ___(5)___ will give you enough of a review to help you remember.

3. Look for Principles. You cannot remember everything. When you try to, you end up remembering nothing. Instead of looking at the assignment as a voluminous collection of ___(6)___ , all of which must be remembered, generalize the subject into a few major ideas, or principles, that you can easily recall. You will find that technique to be especially effective in studying for quizzes and exams.

When you try to remember every last fact in a lesson or a book, you actually ___(7)___ retention and waste time.

(2)		
	praised	worried
forgotten	introduced	nervous

(3)		
	need	hate
want	like	begin

(4)		
	entire	preceding
partial	section	final

(5)		
	statements	questions
skills	announcements	methods

(6)		
	experiences	opinions
facts	goals	results

(7)		
	maximize	ignore
attract	conduct	minimize

Study Skills, Part Two—Read the study skills passage again, paying special attention to the lesson being taught. Then, without looking back at the passage, complete each sentence below by writing in the missing word or words. Check the Answer Key on page 107 for the answers to Study Skills, Part One, and Study Skills, Part Two.

1. If you make an effort and _____ to remember, you will.

2. Most of us have never _____ this simple technique.

3. A good way to prevent forgetting what we read is to _____ the material.

4. To remember important points, repeat the technique of _____ again.

5. Don't try to remember everything. _____ the subject into a few major ideas which you can easily recall.

8 | Narrative of the Life of Frederick Douglass

by Frederick Douglass

Vocabulary—The five words below are from the story you are about to read. Study the words and their meanings. Then complete the ten sentences that follow, using one of the five words to fill in the blank in each sentence. Mark your answer by writing the letter of the word on the line before the sentence. Check your answers in the Answer Key on page 107.

A. **perplexing:** puzzling, confusing

B. **notions:** ideas or concepts

C. **revelation:** a surprising new idea, a revealed truth

D. **diligently:** earnestly, industriously

E. **disposition:** mood, personality, temperament

_____ 1. After she had been forbidden to teach the slave boy, Mrs. Auld's kind _____ changed.

_____ 2. Slavery presented many _____ problems.

_____ 3. The idea that education could be his salvation was a startling _____ to young Frederick.

_____ 4. Day after day, year after year, the slave _____ tried to learn to read.

_____ 5. Complicated _____ about slavery and freedom and right and wrong filled the boy's every waking minute.

_____ 6. Why Mrs. Auld had become tigerlike was a _____ question.

_____ 7. Mr. Auld possessed a strict, even severe, _____ .

_____ 8. With a burning desire to be free, the slave boy _____ worked on his studies.

_____ 9. Despite his circumstances, the boy kept alive _____ of freedom.

_____ 10. In Durgin and Bailey's shipyard came the _____ that he might learn to write.

Why am I a slave? Why are some people slaves, and others masters? Was there ever a time when this was not so? How did the relation commence?

These were the perplexing questions which began now to claim my thoughts, and to exercise the weak powers of my mind, for I was still but a child, and knew less than children of the same age in the free states. As my questions concerning these things were only put to children a little older, and little better informed than myself, I was not rapid in reaching a solid footing. By some means I learned from these inquiries, that "God, up in the sky," made everybody; and that he made white people to be masters and mistresses, and black people to be slaves.

This did not satisfy me, nor lessen my interest in the subject. I was told, too, that God was good, and that He knew what was best for me, and best for everybody. This was less satisfactory than the first statement; because it came, point blank, against all my notions of goodness. It was not good to let old master cut the flesh off Esther, and make her cry so. Besides, how did people know that God made black people to be slaves? Did they go up in the sky and learn it? Or, did He come down and tell them so? All was dark here.

It was some relief to my hard notions of the goodness of God, that, although he made white men to be slave-holders, he did not make them to be bad slaveholders, and that, in due time, he would punish the bad slaveholders; that he would, when they died, send them to the bad place, where they would be "burnt up." Nevertheless, I could not reconcile the relation of slavery with my crude notions of goodness.

Then, too, I found that there were puzzling exceptions to this theory of slavery on both sides, and in the middle. I knew of blacks who were not slaves! I knew of whites who were not slaveholders; and I knew of persons who were nearly white, who were slaves. Color, therefore, was a very unsatisfactory basis for slavery.

Once, however, engaged in the inquiry, I was not very long in finding out the true solution of the matter. It was not color, but crime, not God, but man, that afforded the true explanation of the existence of slavery; nor was I long in finding out another important truth, viz.: what man can make, man can unmake.

The appalling darkness faded away, and I was master of the subject. There were slaves here, direct from Guinea; and there were many who could say that their fathers and mothers were stolen from Africa—forced from their homes, and compelled to serve as slaves. This, to me, was knowledge; but it was a kind of knowledge which filled me with a burning hatred of slavery, increased my suffering, and left me without the means of breaking away from my bondage. Yet it was knowledge quite worth possessing.

I could not have been more than seven or eight years old, when I began to make this subject my study. It was

Mrs. Auld quit teaching Frederick his ABC's when told that such schooling could be bad for the slave owner. But she had already given the boy a taste for learning.

with me in the woods and fields; along the shore of the river, and wherever my boyish wanderings led me; and although I was, at that time, quite ignorant of the existence of the free states, I distinctly remember being, even then, most strongly impressed with the idea of being a free man some day. This cheering assurance was an inborn dream of my human nature—a constant menace to slavery—and one which all the powers of slavery were unable to silence or extinguish.

Very soon after I went to live with Mr. and Mrs. Auld, she very kindly commenced to teach me the A, B, C. After I had learned this, she assisted me in learning to spell words of three or four letters. Just at this point of my progress, Mr. Auld found out what was going on, and at once forbade Mrs. Auld to instruct me further, telling her, among other things, that it was unlawful, as well as unsafe, to teach a slave to read.

To use his own words, further, he said, "If you give a nigger an inch, he will take an ell [a former English unit of length]. A nigger should know nothing but to obey his master—to do as he is told to do. Learning would spoil the best nigger in the world. Now," said he, "if you teach that nigger how to read, there would be no keeping him. It would forever unfit him to be a slave. He would at once become unmanageable, and of no value to his master. As to himself, it could do him no good, but a great deal of harm. It would make him discontented and unhappy."

These words sank deep into my heart, stirred up sentiments within that lay slumbering, and called into existence an entirely new train of thought. It was a new and special revelation, explaining dark and mysterious things, with which my youthful understanding had struggled, but struggled in vain. I now understood what had been to me a most perplexing difficulty—to wit, the white man's power to enslave the black man. It was a grand achievement, and I prized it highly.

Though conscious of the difficulty of learning without a teacher, I set out with high hope, and a fixed purpose, at whatever cost of trouble, to learn how to read. The very decided manner with which he spoke, and strove to impress his wife with the evil consequences of giving me instruction, served to convince me that he was deeply sensible of the truths he was uttering. It gave me the best assurance that I might rely with the utmost confidence on the results which, he said, would flow from teaching me to read.

What he most dreaded, that I most desired. What he most loved, that I most hated. That which to him was a great evil, to be carefully shunned, was to me a great good, to be diligently sought; and the argument which he so warmly urged, against my learning to read, only served to inspire me with a desire and determination to learn.

In learning to read, I owe almost as much to the bitter opposition of my master, as to the kindly aid of my mistress. I acknowledge the benefit of both . . .

My mistress was, as I have said, a kind and tender-hearted woman; and in the simplicity of her soul she commenced, when I first went to live with her, to treat me as she supposed one human being ought to treat another . . . Slavery proved as injurious to her as it did to me . . . Under its influence, the tender heart became stone, and the lamblike disposition gave way to one of tigerlike fierceness.

The first step in her downward course was her ceasing to instruct me. She now commenced to practice her husband's precepts. She finally became even more violent in her opposition than her husband himself. She was not satisfied with simply doing as well as he had commanded; she seemed anxious to do better. Nothing seemed to make her more angry than to see me with a newspaper. She seemed to think that here lay the danger. I have had her rush at me with a face made all up of fury, and snatch from me a newspaper, in a manner that fully revealed her apprehension. She was an apt woman; and a little experience soon demonstrated, to her satisfaction, that education and slavery were incompatible with each other.

From this time I was most narrowly watched. If I was in a separate room any considerable length of time, I was sure to be suspected of having a book, and was at once called to give an account of myself. All this, however, was too late. The first step had been taken. Mistress, in teaching me the alphabet, had given me the inch, and no precaution could prevent me from taking the ell.

The plan which I adopted, and the one by which I was most successful, was that of making friends of all the little white boys whom I met in the street. As many of these as I could, I converted into teachers. With their kindly aid, obtained at different times and in different places, I finally succeeded in learning to read. When I was sent on errands, I always took my book with me, and by doing one part of my errand quickly, I found time to get a lesson before my return. I used also to carry bread with me, enough of which was always in the house, and to which I was always welcome; for I was much better off in this regard than many of the poor white children in our neighborhood. This bread I used to bestow upon the hungry little urchins, who, in return, would give me that more valuable bread of knowledge. . . .

I was now about twelve years old, and the thought of being a slave for life began to bear heavily upon my heart. Just about this time, I got hold of a book entitled *The Columbian Orator.* Every opportunity I got, I used to read this book. Among much of other interesting matter, I found in it a dialogue between a master and his slave. The slave was represented as having run away from his master three times. The dialogue represented the conversation which took place between them, when the slave was retaken the third time.

In this dialogue, the whole argument in behalf of slavery was brought forward by the master, all of which was disposed of by the slave. The slave was made to say some very smart as well as impressive things in reply to his master—things which had the desired though unexpected effect; for the conversation resulted in the voluntary

Born a slave in Maryland in 1817, Frederick Douglass escaped from bondage in 1838 and became a leading figure in the antislavery movement. He gained famed as an antislavery orator, and told his life story in three autobiographies, which he wrote at three different stages of his life.

Douglass traveled to England after the first autobiography was published in 1845. There he continued to speak against slavery and made friends who bought his freedom. Upon returning to the United States in 1847, Douglass founded the antislavery newspaper, the *North Star,* in Rochester, New York. He also discussed the problems of slavery with President Lincoln several times and served as United States minister to Haiti from 1889 to 1891. Douglass died in 1895.

emancipation of the slave on the part of the master. . . .

The idea as to how I might learn to write was suggested to me by being in Durgin and Bailey's shipyard, and frequently seeing the ship carpenters, after hewing, and getting a piece of timber ready for use, write on the timber the name of that part of the ship for which it was intended.

When a piece of timber was intended for the larboard side, it would be marked thus—"L." When a piece was for the starboard side forward, it would be marked thus—"S.F." For larboard aft, it would be marked thus—"L.A." For starboard aft, it would be marked thus—"S.A." I soon learned the names of these letters, and for what they were intended when placed upon a piece of timber in the shipyard. I immediately commenced copying them, and in a short time was able to make the four letters named.

After that, when I met with any boy whom I knew could write, I would tell him I could write as well as he. The next word would be, "I don't believe you. Let me see you try it." I would then make the letters which I had been so fortunate as to learn, and ask him to beat that. In this way I got a good many lessons in writing, which it is quite possible I should never have gotten in any other way.

During this time, my copy-book was the board fence, brick wall, and pavement; my pen and ink was a lump of chalk. With these, I learned mainly how to write. I then commenced and continued copying the Italics on *Webster's Spelling Book,* until I could make them all without looking on the book. By this time, my little Master Thomas had gone to school, and learned how to write, and had written over a number of copybooks. These had been brought home, and shown to some of our near neighbors, and then laid aside. My mistress used to go to class meeting at the Wilk Street meetinghouse every Monday afternoon, and leave me to take care of the house. When left thus, I used to spend the time in writing in the spaces left in Master Thomas's copy-book, copying what he had written. I continued to do this until I could write a hand very similar to that of Master Thomas.

Thus, after a long, tedious effort for years, I finally succeeded in learning how to write.

Starting Time			*Finishing Time*	
Reading Time			*Reading Rate*	
Comprehension			*Vocabulary*	

Comprehension— Read the following questions and statements. For each one, put an *x* in the box before the option that contains the most complete or accurate answer. Check your answers in the Answer Key on page 107.

1. Douglass received most of his instruction from
   - ☐ a. the boys he met on the street.
   - ☐ b. Mrs. Auld.
   - ☐ c. the shipyards.
   - ☐ d. books.

2. Douglass says he owes his ability to read not only to Mrs. Auld's help but also to
   - ☐ a. Mr. Auld's opposition.
   - ☐ b. Durgin and Bailey's shipyard.
   - ☐ c. Mr. Auld's aid.
   - ☐ d. lessons from Master Thomas.

3. The facts in this story are given in
   - ☐ a. numerical order.
   - ☐ b. chronological order.
   - ☐ c. spatial order.
   - ☐ d. alphabetical order.

4. Which of the following best expresses the theme of the selection?
   - ☐ a. Knowledge is power.
   - ☐ b. Slavery is justified.
   - ☐ c. Ignorance is bliss.
   - ☐ d. Knowledge is dangerous.

5. We can see from the story that Douglass was
   - ☐ a. intelligent.
   - ☐ c. sarcastic.
   - ☐ b. humorous.
   - ☐ d. unkind.

6. Douglass learned early in life that education
   - ☐ a. would never be his.
   - ☐ b. was the key to freedom.
   - ☐ c. causes abject poverty.
   - ☐ d. was the reason for slavery.

7. The slave owners denied education to slaves because
   - ☐ a. there were no black schools.
   - ☐ b. the slaves were too busy working to go to school.
   - ☐ c. the whites feared the results of educating the slaves.
   - ☐ d. black people were not considered capable.

8. The selection describes a boy who has
   - ☐ a. a sense of impending doom.
   - ☐ b. bitter resentment.
   - ☐ c. a serene outlook.
   - ☐ d. relentless determination.

9. Which of the following sayings best applies to Mrs. Auld?
   - ☐ a. The pen is mightier than the sword.
   - ☐ b. It is better to give than to receive.
   - ☐ c. Man is the master of his fate.
   - ☐ d. Corruption of good is the worst of corruptions.

10. In Douglass's mind, slavery symbolizes
   - ☐ a. ignorance.
   - ☐ b. knowledge.
   - ☐ c. religion.
   - ☐ d. corruption.

Comprehension Skills	
1. recalling specific facts	6. making a judgment
2. retaining concepts	7. making an inference
3. organizing facts	8. recognizing tone
4. understanding the main idea	9. understanding characters
5. drawing a conclusion	10. appreciation of literary forms

Study Skills, Part One—Following is a passage with blanks where words have been omitted. Next to the passage are groups of five words, one group for each blank. Complete the passage by circling the correct word for each of the blanks.

Signs and Signals

In well-written texts you will find many *signs* that are meant to guide the ___(1)___ . Signs are the most obvious guides. They are different from *signals*, which we will discuss later.

For our purposes, signs refer to the use of numbers and letters to point out the value or the sequence of thoughts. Perhaps the most commonly recognized reading signs

(1)	player	traveler
	reader	writer	driver

are the numbers *1, 2, 3,* and so on. Their roles as indicators of worth or order are readily apparent to most readers. Sometimes they are ___(2)___ by another sign: "There are *three* major causes of baldness." Upon seeing the word *three* the reader knows that numbers will soon follow.

Letters are often used in the same way as numbers. *A, B,* and *C* or *a, b,* and *c* ___(3)___ consistently throughout texts to guide the reader.

In addition to numbers and letters, integral words in the text can work as signs. We often see the words *one, two,* and *three,* or *first, second,* and *third.* They have the same ___(4)___ and importance to the reader, even though they do not stand out in the text the way alpha-numeric signs do.

Still other signs are the phrases *in the first place, in the second place,* and so on. They also serve to inform the reader that numbering is taking place, though the reader may be only partially ___(5)___ of that process. But it is essential that such phrases be in some way numbered by the reader if the ideas they list are to have the significance the author intended.

Signs are more likely to appear in certain ___(6)___ in the chapter. Often they are used at the beginning to list the important elements to be covered.

Another place to look for signs is at the end of a chapter or section. There they are used as a summary listing of ___(7)___ elements discussed in the preceding material.

| (2) | followed | delivered |
| | inserted | presented | introduced |

| (3) | sustain | appear |
| | vanish | count | gain |

| (4) | value | price |
| | reason | standard | benefit |

| (5) | fond | thankful |
| | approving | grateful | aware |

| (6) | methods | ways |
| | places | periods | patterns |

| (7) | important | unknown |
| | distinguished | instant | stately |

Study Skills, Part Two—Read the study skills passage again, paying special attention to the lesson being taught. Then, without looking back at the passage, complete each sentence below by writing in the missing word or words. Check the Answer Key on page 107 for the answers to Study Skills, Part One, and Study Skills, Part Two.

1. Signs are such _____ guides that we separate them from signals.

2. Signs refer to the use of numbers and _____ to point out important ideas.

3. Also used as signs are words and phrases. For example, we may see the word *fourth* used instead of the number _____ .

4. Signs are often found at the _____ of the chapter, listing important things to come.

5. Signs are also found at the end of the chapter where they are used to list _____ of important ideas.

The Boy Who Painted Christ Black

by John Henrik Clarke

Vocabulary—The five words below are from the story you are about to read. Study the words and their meanings. Then complete the ten sentences that follow, using one of the five words to fill in the blank in each sentence. Mark your answer by writing the letter of the word on the line before the sentence. Check your answers in the Answer Key on page 107.

A. profound: deeply felt

B. submerged: covered over or hidden just below the surface

C. coherent: logical, clear, consistent

D. array: orderly arrangement

E. immune: exempt, free

_____ 1. The _____ of artwork was an impressive testament to the talent of all the students.

_____ 2. Professor Danual's feelings of anger were too strong to remain _____ for long.

_____ 3. No student was _____ to the teacher's reproachful glare.

_____ 4. Because Christ had such a _____ feeling of kindness, Aaron felt he must have been a black man.

_____ 5. The teacher was so overwhelmed by Aaron's gift that she was incapable of _____ speech.

_____ 6. Visitors were treated to an _____ of colorful works that stretched from one end of the room to the other.

_____ 7. The _____ outrage that Professor Danual felt was quite evident as he questioned Aaron.

_____ 8. An undercurrent of barely _____ fright swept through the auditorium as Professor Danual made his way to the front of the room.

_____ 9. Aaron's second attempt at an explanation was more _____ than the first.

_____ 10. No one was _____ to the tension caused by Professor Danual's visit.

He was the smartest boy in the Muskogee County School—for colored children. Everybody even remotely connected with the school knew this. The teacher always pronounced his name with profound gusto as she pointed him out as the ideal student. Once I heard her say: "If he were white he might, some day, become President." Only Aaron Crawford wasn't white; quite the contrary. His skin was so solid black that it glowed, reflecting an inner virtue that was strange, and beyond my comprehension.

His great variety of talent often startled the teachers. This caused his classmates to look upon him with a mixed feeling of awe and envy.

Before Thanksgiving, he always drew turkeys and pumpkins on the blackboard. On George Washington's birthday, he drew large American flags surrounded by little hatchets. It was these small masterpieces that made him the most talked-about colored boy in Columbus, Georgia. The Negro principal of the Muskogee County School said he would some day be a great painter, like Henry O. Tanner.

For the teacher's birthday, which fell on a day about a week before commencement, Aaron Crawford painted the picture that caused an uproar, and a turning point, at the Muskogee County School. The moment he entered the room that morning, all eyes fell on him. Besides his torn book holder, he was carrying a large-framed concern wrapped in old newspapers. As he went to his seat, the teacher's eyes followed his every motion, a curious wonderment mirrored in them conflicting with the half-smile that wreathed her face.

Aaron put his books down, then smiling broadly, advanced toward the teacher's desk.

Already the teacher sensed that Aaron had a present for her. Still smiling, he placed it on her desk and began to help her unwrap it. As the last piece of paper fell from the large frame, the teacher jerked her hand away from it suddenly, her eyes flickering unbelievingly. Amidst the rigid tension, her heavy breathing was distinct and frightening. Temporarily, there was no other sound in the room.

With a quick, involuntary movement I rose up from my desk. A series of submerged murmurs spread through the room, rising to a distinct monotone. The teacher turned toward the children, staring reproachfully. They did not move their eyes from the present that Aaron had brought her. . . . It was a large picture of Christ—painted black!

Aaron Crawford went back to his seat, a feeling of triumph reflecting in his every movement.

The teacher faced us.

"Aaron," she spoke at last, a slight tinge of uncertainty in her tone, "this is a most welcome present. Thanks. I will treasure it." She paused, then went on speaking, a trifle more coherent than before. "Looks like you are going to be quite an artist. . . . Suppose you come forward

The principal knew that Aaron's painting would cause trouble, but he let Aaron display it anyway. Perhaps the principal wanted a chance to speak his mind.

and tell the class how you came to paint this remarkable picture."

When he rose to speak, to explain about the picture, a hush fell tightly over the room, and the children gave him all of their attention . . . something they rarely did for the teacher. He did not speak at first; he just stood there in front of the room, toying absently with his hands, observing his audience carefully, like a great concert artist.

"It was like this," he said, placing full emphasis on every word. "You see, my uncle who lives in New York teaches classes in Negro History at the Y.M.C.A. When he visited us last year he was telling me about the many great black folks who have made history. He said black folks were once the most powerful people on earth. When I asked him about Christ, he said no one ever proved whether he was black or white. Somehow a feeling came over me that he was a black man, 'cause he was so kind and forgiving, kinder than I have ever seen white people be. So, when I painted his picture I couldn't help but paint it as I thought it was."

After this, the little artist sat down, smiling broadly, as if he had gained entrance to a great storehouse of knowledge that ordinary people could neither acquire nor comprehend.

The teacher, knowing nothing else to do under prevailing circumstances, invited the children to rise from their seats and come forward so they could get a complete view of Aaron's unique piece of art.

When I came close to the picture, I noticed it was painted with the kind of paint you get in the five and ten cent stores. Its shape was blurred slightly, as if someone had jarred the frame before the paint had time to dry. The eyes of Christ were deepset and sad, very much like those of Aaron's father, who was a deacon in the local Baptist Church. This picture of Christ looked much different from the one I saw hanging on the wall when I was in Sunday School. It looked more like a helpless Negro, pleading silently for mercy.

For the next few days, there was much talk about Aaron's picture.

The school term ended the following week and Aaron's picture, along with the best handwork done by the students that year, was on display in the assembly room. Naturally, Aaron's picture graced the place of honor.

In the middle of the day all the children were gathered in the small assembly. On this day we were always favored with a visit from a man whom all the teachers spoke of with mixed esteem and fear. Professor Danual, they called him, and they always pronounced his name with reverence. He was supervisor of all the city schools, including those small and poorly equipped ones set aside for colored children.

The great man arrived almost at the end of our commencement exercises. On seeing him enter the hall, the children rose, bowed courteously, and sat down again, their eyes examining him as if he were a circus freak.

He was a tall white man with solid gray hair that made his lean face seem paler than it actually was. His eyes were the clearest blue I have ever seen. They were the only life-like things about him.

As he made his way to the front of the room the Negro principal, George Du Vaul, was walking ahead of him, cautiously preventing anything from getting in his way. As he passed me, I heard the teachers, frightened, sucking in their breath, felt the tension tightening.

A large chair was in the center of the rostrum. It had been daintily polished and the janitor had laboriously recushioned its bottom. The supervisor went straight to it without being guided, knowing that this pretty splendor was reserved for him.

Presently the Negro principal introduced the distinguished guest and he favored us with a short speech. It wasn't a very important speech. Almost at the end of it, I remember him saying something about he wouldn't be surprised if one of us boys grew up to be a great colored man, like Booker T. Washington.

After he sat down, the school chorus sang two spirituals and the girls in the fourth grade did an Indian folk dance. This brought the commencement program to an end.

After this the supervisor came down from the rostrum, his eyes tinged with curiosity, and began to view the array of handwork on display in front of the chapel.

Suddenly his face underwent a strange rejuvenation. His clear blue eyes flickered in astonishment. He was looking at Aaron Crawford's picture of Christ. Mechanically he moved his stooped form closer to the picture and stood gazing fixedly at it, curious and undecided, as though it were a dangerous animal that would rise any moment and spread destruction.

"Who painted this sacrilegious nonsense?" he demanded sharply.

"I painted it, sir." These were Aaron's words, spoken hesitantly. He wetted his lips timidly and looked up at the supervisor, his eyes voicing a sad plea for understanding.

He spoke again, this time more coherently. "Th' principal said a colored person have jes as much right paintin' Jesus black as a white person have paintin' him white. An he says. . . ." At this point he halted abruptly, as if to search for his next words. A strong tinge of bewilderment dimmed the glow of his solid black face. He stammered out a few more words, then stopped again.

The supervisor strode a few steps toward him. At last color had swelled some of the lifelessness out his lean face.

"Well, go on!" he said, enragedly, ". . . I'm listening."

Aaron moved his lips pathetically but no words passed them. His eyes wandered around the room, resting finally, with an air of hope, on the face of the Negro principal. After a moment, he jerked his face in another direction, regretfully, as if something he had said had betrayed an understanding between him and the principal.

Presently the principal stepped forward to defend the school's prize student.

"I encouraged the boy in painting that picture," he said firmly. "And it was with my permission that he brought the picture into this school. I don't think the boy is so far wrong in painting Christ black. The artists of all other races have painted whatsoever God they worship to resemble themselves. I see no reason why we should be immune from that privilege. After all, Christ was born in that part of the world that had always been predominantly populated by colored people. There is a strong possibility that he could have been a Negro."

The supervisor swallowed dumfoundedly. His face was aglow in silent rage.

"Have you been teaching these children things like that?" he asked the Negro principal, sternly.

"I have been teaching them that their race has produced great kings and queens as well as slaves and serfs," the principal said. "The time is long overdue when we should let the world know that we erected and enjoyed the benefits of a splendid civilization long before the people of Europe had a written language."

The supervisor coughed. His eyes bulged menacingly as he spoke. "You are not being paid to teach such things in this school, and I am demanding your resignation for overstepping your limit as principal."

George Du Vaul did not speak. A strong quiver swept over his sullen face. He revolved himself slowly and walked out of the room towards his office.

The supervisor's eyes followed him until he was out of focus. Then he murmured under his breath: "There'll be a lot of fuss in this world if you start people thinking that Christ was a nigger."

Some of the teachers followed the principal out of the chapel, leaving the crestfallen children restless and in a quandary about what to do next. Finally, we started back to our rooms. The supervisor was behind me. I heard him murmur to himself: "Damn, if niggers ain't getting smarter."

A few days later I heard that the principal had accepted a summer job as art instructor of a small high school somewhere in south Georgia and had gotten permission from Aaron's parents to take him along so he could continue to encourage him in his painting.

I was on my way home when I saw him leaving his office. He was carrying a large briefcase and some books tucked under his arm. He had already said good-by to all the teachers. And strangely, he did not look brokenhearted. As he headed for the large front door, he readjusted his horn-rimmed glasses, but did not look back. An air of triumph gave more dignity to his soldierly stride. He had the appearance of a man who had done a great thing, something greater than any ordinary man would do.

Aaron Crawford was waiting outside for him. They walked down the street together. He put his arms around Aaron's shoulder affectionately. He was talking sincerely to Aaron about something, and Aaron was listening, deeply earnest.

I watched them until they were so far down the street that their forms had begun to blur. Even from this distance I could see they were still walking in brisk, dignified strides, like two people who had won some sort of victory.

A graduate of New York University, John Henrik Clarke was the first teacher of African-American history to be licensed in New York state. He created the "Black Heritage" history series for CBS, and has won several awards for his television work.

Clarke is well known for his work as a writer and editor. His book of poetry, *Rebellion in Rhyme,* followed a World-War II experience as a master sergeant. Clarke co-founded the *Harlem Quarterly* and worked for several other black newspapers. He is also a co-founder of the Black Academy of Arts and Letters.

Starting Time		Finishing Time	
Reading Time		Reading Rate	
Comprehension		Vocabulary	

Comprehension— Read the following questions and statements. For each one, put an *x* in the box before the option that contains the most complete or accurate answer. Check your answers in the Answer Key on page 107.

1. Aaron lived in
   □ a. Louisiana.
   □ b. Florida.
   □ c. Mississippi.
   □ d. Georgia.

2. Aaron felt that, compared to black people, white people were
   □ a. intelligent and cultured.
   □ b. unkind and unforgiving.
   □ c. humble and tolerant.
   □ d. unclean and poor.

3. At what point in Aaron's life does this story take place?
   □ a. during his childhood
   □ b. during his teen years
   □ c. during middle age
   □ d. in his old age

4. The selection illustrates which of the following?
   □ a. The truth shall set you free.
   □ b. The meek shall inherit the earth.
   □ c. Pride goeth before destruction.
   □ d. The evil that men do lives after them.

5. What was Aaron's religion?
   □ a. Catholic
   □ b. Episcopalian
   □ c. Baptist
   □ d. Mormon

6. Aaron's black Christ represented
   □ a. the historically oppressed black.
   □ b. the influence of the principal.
   □ c. the black man's dream of a better future.
   □ d. his efforts at creativity.

7. The teacher's first reaction to Aaron's painting resulted from
   □ a. ignorance.
   □ b. misunderstanding.
   □ c. fear.
   □ d. intolerance.

8. As the principal and Aaron walked away from the school, they had an air of
   □ a. relief and unconcern.
   □ b. victory in apparent defeat.
   □ c. complete defeat.
   □ d. cockiness and arrogance.

9. The principal's character can be described as
   □ a. courageous.
   □ b. creative.
   □ c. deceptive.
   □ d. diplomatic.

10. The narrator of the selection is
   □ a. a teacher.
   □ b. a student.
   □ c. an administrator.
   □ d. the principal.

Comprehension Skills

1. recalling specific facts
2. retaining concepts
3. organizing facts
4. understanding the main idea
5. drawing a conclusion
6. making a judgment
7. making an inference
8. recognizing tone
9. understanding characters
10. appreciation of literary forms

Study Skills, Part One—Following is a passage with blanks where words have been omitted. Next to the passage are groups of five words, one group for each blank. Complete the passage by circling the correct word for each of the blanks.

Forward Signals

Signals are useful guides for the reader, but they are not as apparent as signs. The first types of signals that we are going to look at are called Forward Signals.

This group of signals tells the reader to ___(1)___ with the thought. They indicate that more of the same is coming and that the reader should continue forward.

The most common forward signals are *and, more, moreover, more than that, furthermore, also,* and *likewise.*

The most frequently used word in that group is *and.* It is a forward signal that tells the reader that another item of ___(2)___ importance will follow or that the items are parts of a series. It tells you that you will not be faced with an ___(3)___ or reversing thought—you can go right on for more of the same.

The signals *more, moreover, more than that,* and *furthermore* all indicate that new and even stronger thoughts are coming up: "She's clever all right; *more than that,* she's a genius." It is plain how such signals strengthen and add depth to the ___(4)___ idea.

The signal *likewise* means "in the same manner." *Also,* by the same token, indicates that statements of ideas quite ___(5)___ to those that have preceded are about to follow: "Along with signs, authors *also* use signals." Signals are unlike signs in many ways. Signs, as you recall, stand out in the text; most of them are easy to ___(6)___ . In fact, they are nearly impossible to miss. Signs are usually placed above or in front of the numbered material.

Signals, on the other hand, are words, and they are woven into the text. They are not set apart from the rest of the copy. For that reason, they are not as easy to spot as signs, and they therefore require the reader to be ___(7)___ for their appearance and function.

(1)	advance	finish
	endure	insist	end

(2)	rival	equal
	vast	primary	greater

(3)	opposing	easy
	obvious	essential	aggressive

(4)	following	final
	future	previous	different

(5)	different	similar
	advanced	contrasting	simple

(6)	study	refer
	employ	identify	repeat

(7)	present	alert
	eager	restless	absent

Study Skills, Part Two—Read the study skills passage again, paying special attention to the lesson being taught. Then, without looking back at the passage, complete each sentence below by writing in the missing word or words. Check the Answer Key on page 107 for the answers to Study Skills, Part One, and Study Skills, Part Two.

1. Other words that _____ the reader are called signals.

2. Signals are more _____ to find than signs because they do not stand out from the rest of the text.

3. The signals in the first group tell the reader to continue. They are called _____ signals.

4. The signal word *and* is the most common. It joins items of equal importance or items in a _____.

5. The words *more* and *moreover* are _____ signal words. They tell the reader that the items to follow will add to the original idea.

10 | # How to Win at Basketball: Cheat

by Bill Cosby

Vocabulary—The five words below are from the story you are about to read. Study the words and their meanings. Then complete the ten sentences that follow, using one of the five words to fill in the blank in each sentence. Mark your answer by writing the letter of the word on the line before the sentence. Check your answers in the Answer Key on page 107.

A. impartial: fair to all concerned

B. free: unobstructed; clear

C. fake: employ a false or deceptive move

D. strange: unfamiliar

E. earned: having gained something by proving one's worth

_____ 1. One good basketball move was to face your opponent and _____ a move.

_____ 2. If you got the ball but couldn't shoot it, the best thing to do was to pass it to a _____ team member.

_____ 3. The referees in a basketball game must remain _____ at all times.

_____ 4. Most good players on the playground _____ themselves a nickname.

_____ 5. When you were unsure of what to do next, a _____ was a good idea.

_____ 6. Since each fan had a favorite team it was hard for them to remain _____ .

_____ 7. Only after long arguments were points _____ in this game.

_____ 8. Playing on a _____ court was not always the best of situations.

_____ 9. The balcony blocked the ball on one side of the court, so the players moved to the _____ side.

_____ 10. The multi-colored uniforms were uncommon and _____ .

When I played basketball in the slums of Philadelphia—outdoors on concrete courts—there was never a referee. You had to call your own fouls. So the biggest argument was always about whether you called the foul *before* the shot went in, or whether you had waited to see if the ball went in. See, if you yelled "foul," you didn't get the basket. You just got the ball out-of-bounds.

Sometimes you called a *light* foul. Like you have a guy driving in on you and you punch him in the eye a little. That's a light foul in the playgrounds.

Another light foul is submarining a guy who's driving in on you. He comes down on the concrete, and you visit him every two weeks in the hospital. Of course, there is always a pole sitting in the middle of the court. Something has to hold up the basket. So you let a guy drive in, and you just kind of screen him a little bit, right into the pole. This is where you visit him three times a week in the hospital.

There's always a big argument, too, about whether you stepped out-of-bounds or not. That's a four-hour argument. So usually you take one shot—20-minute argument. Another shot—20-minute argument. Out-of-bounds—four-hour argument. So this one game—the winner is the first team to score 20 points—can go maybe two weeks. The most important thing is to remember the score from day to day. Sometimes you argue four hours about *that.*

To play on any team outdoors, you have to have a pair of old jeans that you cut off and shred a little bit above the knees so they look like beachcomber pants. You get an old sweat shirt of some university—mine was Temple—and you go outside to the playground, and play basketball all day, until dark, and your mother has to come get you.

Let me say something about mothers. When I was a kid, mothers were never really interested in sports. Even if you became a fantastic star, your mother was probably the last person to know. She was more concerned with you being on time for dinner.

My mother was a fantastic color changer. Whatever color my uniform was, my mother would always put it into the washing machine with different-colored stuff—the red bedspread, the green curtains, the yellow tablecloth, or the purple bathroom rug. And when the uniform came out, instead of being white it would be avocado.

I've worn a pink uniform, and I've worn a running yellow-and-blue uniform—which of course startled my teammates quite a bit. One time, I had to learn karate in order to answer for a pale-lavender uniform.

Later, I graduated from playground basketball to indoor basketball. I played for a place called the Wissahickon Boys' Club along with a very famous defensive back by the name of Herb Adderley.

Well, very few teams could whip the Wissahickon Boys'

The rules of the game, Cosby-style, from ol' weird Harold and the gang in the slums of Philadelphia to Celebrity Basketball in the fabulous Forum.

Club on our own court, mainly because our court was different. First of all, the floor hadn't been varnished and the out-of-bounds lines hadn't been painted since the day the gym was built, about two weeks after Dr. Naismith invented basketball. We didn't have to see them. We could feel where they were. Our sneakers had soles as thick as a piece of paper. But it was hell on the other team.

So was the ball. We used a leather ball that had been played with outside—in the dark of night, in the rain, in the snow. It was about as heavy as a medicine ball, and just as lively. There were stones and pieces of glass stuck into it, and it never had enough air, because the valve leaked. You could wear yourself out just trying to dribble it.

Now about the basket. The rim was loose, and hanging, and shaking. And all you had to do was kind of lay that heavy ball up softly. The rim acted like a trampoline. It lifted the ball up and threw it through the center of the hoop and you always had two points.

Another thing about playing at the Wissahickon Boys' Club. We would get ol' Weird Harold, who was six feet nine and weighed about 90 pounds, to mark black X's all over the backboard. Now, only our team knew what each X stood for. See, we aimed maybe two inches under a mark, and, zap, two points. If you followed our mark, you'd miss the rim. We always had something going for ourselves.

The ceiling in the gym was only fifteen feet high. For those who may not know that much about basketball, that means our ceiling was only five feet above the rim of the basket itself. When other teams came to play us, they weren't aware right away that the ceiling was low. So when they shot the ball, they hit the ceiling—which was out-of-bounds. And we would get the ball. Meanwhile, we had practiced shooting our jump shots and set shots on a direct line drive. No arch, no nothing—just straight ahead into the basket. Sort of Woody Sauldsberry style.

We also had a hot-water pipe that ran around the wall, and the wall of the gym was out-of-bounds. So whenever a guy on the other team would go up for a rebound or a jump shot, or drive into the basket, we would kind of screen him into the hot-water pipe.

At the Wissahickon Boys' Club, we had graduated to the point where we had referees for the games. We had them because they were honest and fair and impartial. Which is what they teach at boys' clubs. Also because we were playing teams from other neighborhoods and had to finish the games in one day. The referees cut down on the long arguments.

We had two steady refs whom we named Mr. Magoo and The Bat. You might say they did not have Superman vision. They more or less had to make their calls on what they could hear. Like if they heard a slap, and thought they saw the ball fly out of a guy's hands, they cried "foul" for hacking. So whenever a guy would go up for a rebound or something, all we had to do was just give him a little nudge, and boom! He'd wind up against the wall and probably that hot-water pipe. His screams would tell The Bat and Mr. Magoo he was out-of-bounds.

When new teams came down to play us and saw our uniforms, which consisted of heavy old long-sleeved flannel pajama tops over below-the-knee corduroy knickers, they'd call us "turkeys" and all kinds of chicken names. Maybe we weren't cool. But we were protected from that hot-water pipe.

One time, Cryin' Charlie's mother had his PJ tops in the washing machine at game time, and we had to make him non-playing coach that day so he wouldn't cry.

In the middle of the court, we had five boards that happened to be about the loosest boards that you ever stepped on in your life. So that while dribbling downcourt on a fast break, if you hit one of those five boards, the ball would not come back to you. Many times, a guy on the other team would dribble downcourt on the fast break, and all of a sudden he'd be running, and his arm would be pumping, but there was no ball coming back up to him. All we had to do was just stand at the loose boards, and without even stickin' the guy, let him go ahead and do his Lamont Cranston dribble, and we could pick up the ball, dead and waiting, right there. Whenever *we* went on a fast break, we dribbled *around* those loose boards.

One team I remember we lost to was the Nicetown Club for Boys & Girls. We played in their gym. They had a balcony that extended out over one side of the court about ten feet. It was almost exactly the same height as the rim of the basket. So if you went up for a jumper, the balcony would block your shot. The defense of the Nicetown Club was to force the flow of your offense to the side of the court with the balcony. When we tried to shoot from there, the Bill Russell balcony would block the shot, and the ball would bounce back and hit our man in the eye. Whenever *they* came downcourt, they would play on the free side of the floor away from the balcony.

I would say, on a home-and-home basis, the Wissahickon Boys' Club and the Nicetown Club were even.

In high school, I had one of the greatest jump shots— from two feet out—anybody ever saw. The only man who stopped me was Wilt Chamberlain.

We played Wilt's high school, Overbrook, and they had a guy on the team by the name of Ira Davis, who was a great track man. He ran the 100 in like nine-point-some-thing, and few years later was in the Olympic Games. Ira was great on the fast break. So Chamberlain would stand under our basket and growl at us. And when he growled, guys would just throw the ball at him—to try and hit him with it. And he would catch it and throw it downcourt

Bill Cosby is best known for his hit television series "The Cosby Show," his stand-up comedy act and comedy albums, and numerous television commercials.
   Bill Cosby received a doctorate in education from the University of Massachusetts in 1977. He has been married for over twenty years and has five children.

to Ira Davis, who would score 200 points on the fast break. We lost to them something like 800 to 14. My best shot was where I would dribble in quickly, stop, fake the man playing me into the air, and then go up for my two-foot jump shot. Well, I was very surprised when I found Mr. Chamberlain waiting under the basket for me; I faked, and faked and faked and faked and faked, and then I threw the ball at him and tried to hit him. But he caught it and threw it downcourt to Ira Davis: 802 to 14.

So then we tried to razzle-dazzle him. But for some reason, he could always follow the ball with that one eye of his in the middle of his forehead. And of course, the only thing we could do was just throw the ball at him.

We had one play we used on Wilt that had some success. We had one kid that was completely crazy. He wasn't afraid of anything in the world. Not even the Big Dipper. He was about as big as Mickey Rooney, and we had him run out on the court and punch Chamberlain right in the kneecap. And when Chamberlain bent over to grab our guy, we shot our jumpers. That foul alone was worth our 14 points.

Now that I'm a celebrity making a million dollars a year, we have Celebrity Basketball. I play with guys like James Garner, Jim Brown, Don Adams, Sidney Poitier, Mike Connors, Mickey Rooney, and Jack Lemmon.

In Celebrity Basketball, you pull up to the fabulous Forum in your Rolls-Royce, and your chauffeur puts you in a beach chair and wheels you out on the court. And after each shot, you have a catered affair.

And the ball. The pros wish they could find a ball this great. It's gold covered and has a little transistor motor inside, with radar and a homing device, and it dribbles and shoots itself.

A sixty-piece orchestra plays background music while you're down on the court, and starlet cheerleaders are jumping up and down. After every basket, we all stop and give the guy who scored it a standing ovation.

Another thing about when I used to play basketball in the playgrounds. If you went to a strange playground, you didn't introduce yourself. You had to prove yourself first. No names.

"Over here, my man."

"Yeah, nice play, my man."

Later on, if you earned it, you'd be given a name: Gunner, My Man, or Herman or Shorty or something.

Now, when we play the Celebrity games, they come

out on the court and say, "Hi, my name is such and such. I'm from so forth and so on," and the whole thing. And I say, "Oh, very nice to meet you."

But later, during the game, I forget the cat's name anyway and I just go right back to "Over here, my man. I'm free in the corner, my man." And I'm back in the old neighborhood.

Starting Time		Finishing Time	
Reading Time		Reading Rate	
Comprehension		Vocabulary	

Comprehension — Read the following questions and statements. For each one, put an *x* in the box before the option that contains the most complete or accurate answer. Check your answers in the Answer Key on page 107.

1. Bill Cosby grew up in
   - ☐ a. New York City.
   - ☐ b. Chicago.
   - ☐ c. Boston.
   - ☐ d. Philadelphia.

2. Bill Cosby says that, in general,
   - ☐ a. mothers are not interested in their sons' athletic pursuits.
   - ☐ b. a sixty-piece orchestra plays good background music.
   - ☐ c. celebrity basketball is a good fund-raiser in Hollywood.
   - ☐ d. playing basketball in the slums was not much fun.

3. In this selection, Cosby is
   - ☐ a. discussing plans for the future.
   - ☐ b. reliving his childhood.
   - ☐ c. preaching before a crowd.
   - ☐ d. predicting the black man's fate.

4. Which of the following best expresses Cosby's feelings about Celebrity Basketball?
   - ☐ a. As riches grow, cares follow.
   - ☐ b. It is better to live rich than to die rich.
   - ☐ c. Eat with the rich, but play with the poor, who are capable of joy.
   - ☐ d. Simple pleasures, remembered with fondness, have no counterpart that money can buy.

5. The crazy kid punched Chamberlain in the knee. To Cosby and his teammates this was just another example of
   - ☐ a. poor sportsmanship.
   - ☐ b. the end justifying the means.
   - ☐ c. incompetent refereeing.
   - ☐ d. erratic behavior.

6. The last part of the story leads us to believe that
   - ☐ a. celebrities do not like basketball.
   - ☐ b. not all celebrities drive expensive cars.
   - ☐ c. basketball requires much skill.
   - ☐ d. Cosby misses the old neighborhood.

7. Bill Cosby would probably be the first to admit that his mother was
   - ☐ a. a sports fan.
   - ☐ b. a good cook.
   - ☐ c. color blind.
   - ☐ d. his best fan.

8. In relating this story Bill Cosby relies largely upon
   - ☐ a. opinions.
   - ☐ b. research.
   - ☐ c. suspense.
   - ☐ d. humor.

9. An outstanding characteristic of the Wissahickon team was its
   - ☐ a. brutality.
   - ☐ b. humor.
   - ☐ c. inventiveness.
   - ☐ d. solidarity.

10. "We lost to them something like 800 to 14." That sentence shows the use of
   - ☐ a. sarcasm.
   - ☐ b. exaggeration.
   - ☐ c. irony.
   - ☐ d. personification.

Comprehension Skills	
1. recalling specific facts	6. making a judgment
2. retaining concepts	7. making an inference
3. organizing facts	8. recognizing tone
4. understanding the main idea	9. understanding characters
5. drawing a conclusion	10. appreciation of literary forms

Study Skills, Part One—Following is a passage with blanks where words have been omitted. Next to the passage are groups of five words, one group for each blank. Complete the passage by circling the correct word for each of the blanks.

Summary Signals

We have already seen some signals that appear in the text to encourage the reader to move forward because more ideas of the same kind are coming. As you will recall, they are called Forward Signals.

Other signals that also __(1)__ the reader forward are called Summary Signals.

They are also Forward Signals, but we put them in their own group because the __(2)__ they do is much more specific. They signal not only that the thought is going on, but also that a new idea is being introduced. The new idea will be one of summary or consequence.

Words such as *thus, therefore, consequently,* and *accordingly* tell the reader that the author is not only advancing the first thought but is also introducing an added one. That added idea will wrap up what has already been said or will reveal the __(3)__ of earlier ideas. The reader, alerted by the signal words to the new idea, is made aware that the author has been leading up to a synthesis of the original and the new ideas. At that point, the writer will, ideally __(4)__ and summarize the complete thought and show the result or effect it has caused.

The word *thus* is a Summary Signal. It tells the reader that what follows is not simply more of the same, but is a thought carrying greater __(5)__ for the reader.

In textbooks especially, Summary Signals __(6)__ ideas and concepts the author feels are of great importance.

Frequently, Summary Signals appear at the beginning of __(7)__ that summarize the writer's presentation.

(1)   urge   force
     halt   teach   thrust

(2)   fortune   spot
     job   career   business

(3)   result   reason
     subject   source   origin

(4)   pause   decrease
     extend   minimize   create

(5)   meaning   expression
     motion   enjoyment   involvement

(6)   identify   ignore
     include   contain   discard

(7)   ideas   questions
     statements   reports   opinions

Study Skills, Part Two—Read the study skills passage again, paying special attention to the lesson being taught. Then, without looking back at the passage, complete each sentence below by writing in the missing word or words. Check the Answer Key on page 107 for the answers to Study Skills, Part One, and Study Skills, Part Two.

1. Summary Signals are a special kind of Forward Signal, because they present the reader with a _____ idea.

2. Summary Signals, therefore, have a job that is more _____ than other Forward Signals.

3. Summary Signals tell the reader that the author has _____ presenting his ideas and is about to state the result or conclusion.

4. In _____ especially, these signals introduce important conclusions by the author.

5. Summary Signals usually appear at the _____ of the author's summary.

A Raisin in the Sun

by Lorraine Hansberry

Vocabulary—The five words below are from the story you are about to read. Study the words and their meanings. Then complete the ten sentences that follow, using one of the five words to fill in the blank in each sentence. Mark your answer by writing the letter of the word on the line before the sentence. Check your answers in the Answer Key on page 107.

A. amiably: with friendliness

B. minor: lesser or smaller

C. labored: lacking ease; bearing the characteristics of effort

D. deplore: to regret deeply

E. quizzical: questioning, inquisitive

_____ 1. Beneatha stopped what she was doing and turned a _____ stare upon the visitor.

_____ 2. Mr. Lindner's _____ breathing told of his nervous anxiety about the meeting.

_____ 3. Although he spoke _____, Mr. Lindner concealed a deeper, more malevolent feeling.

_____ 4. Mr. Lindner's first statements caused Ruth and Walter to exchange _____ glances.

_____ 5. Mr. Lindner's _____ nervous activity did not go undetected by Beneatha.

_____ 6. The feelings of the people of Clybourne Park could not be considered _____ concerns.

_____ 7. Mr. Lindner explained that the people of Clybourne Park would _____ having black people in the neighborhood.

_____ 8. As he gathered the courage to speak frankly, Mr. Lindner's actions were _____.

_____ 9. Upon meeting Mr. Lindner, Walter _____ asked if he wanted a beer.

_____ 10. "I _____ the fact that I am the bearer of such news," Mr. Lindner informed his audience.

(Beneatha goes to the door and opens it as Walter and Ruth go on with the clowning. Beneatha is somewhat surprised to see a quiet-looking middle-aged white man in a business suit holding his hat and a briefcase in his hand and consulting a small piece of paper)

Man: Uh—how do you do, miss. I am looking for a Mrs.—*(He looks at the slip of paper)* Mrs. Lena Younger?

Beneatha *(Smoothing her hair with slight embarrassment)*: Oh—yes, that's my mother. Excuse me. *(She closes the door and turns to quiet the other two)* Ruth! Brother! Somebody's here.

(Then she opens the door. The man casts a curious quick glance at all of them) Uh—come in, please.

Man *(Coming in)*: Thank you.

Beneatha: My mother isn't here just now. Is it business?

Man: Yes . . . well, of a sort.

Walter *(Freely, the Man of the House)*: Have a seat. I'm Mrs. Younger's son. I look after most of her business matters.

(Ruth and Beneatha exchange amused glances)

Man *(Regarding Walter, and sitting)*: Well—My name is Karl Lindner . . .

Walter *(Stretching out his hand)*: Walter Younger. This is my wife—*(Ruth nods politely)*—and my sister.

Lindner: How do you do.

Walter *(Amiably, as he sits himself easily on a chair, leaning with interest forward on his knees and looking expectantly into the newcomer's face)*: What can we do for you, Mr. Lindner?

Lindner *(Some minor shuffling of the hat and briefcase on his knees)*: Well—I am a representative of the Clybourne Park Improvement Association—

Walter *(Pointing)*: Why don't you sit your things on the floor?

Lindner Oh—yes. Thank you. *(He slides the briefcase and hat under the chair)* And as I was saying—I am from the Clybourne Park Improvement Association and we have had it brought to our attention at the last meeting that you people—or at least your mother—has bought a piece of residential property at—*(He digs for the slip of paper again)*—four o six Clybourne Street. . .

Walter: That's right. Care for something to drink? Ruth, get Mr. Lindner a beer.

Lindner *(Upset for some reason)*: Oh—no, really. I mean thank you very much, but no thank you.

Ruth *(Innocently)*: Some coffee?

Lindner Thank you, nothing at all. *(Beneatha is watching the man carefully)*

The man dropped in on the Younger family to avert trouble. But behind the bland statement of his concern lurked a message distorted by hate and fear.

Lindner Well, I don't know how much you folks know about our organization. *(He's a gentle man; thoughtful and somewhat labored in his manner)* It is one of these community organizations set up to look after—oh, you know, things like block upkeep and special projects and we also have what we call our New Neighbors Orientation Committee. . .

Beneatha *(Drily)*: Yes—and what do they do?

Lindner *(Turning a little to her and then returning the main force to Walter)*: Well—It's what you might call a sort of welcoming committee, I guess. I mean they, we, I'm the chairman of the committee—go around and see the new people who move into the neighborhood and sort of give them the lowdown on the way we do things out in Clybourne Park.

Beneatha *(With appreciation of the two meanings, which escape Ruth and Walter)*: Un-huh.

Lindner: And we also have the category of what the association calls—*(He looks elsewhere)*—uh—special community problems. . .

Beneatha: Yes—and what are some of those?

Walter: Girl, let the man talk.

Lindner *(With understated relief)*: Thank you. I would sort of like to explain this thing in my own way. I mean I want to explain to you in a certain way.

Walter: Go ahead.

Lindner Yes. Well. I'm going to try to get right to the point. I'm sure we'll all appreciate that in the long run.

Beneatha: Yes.

Walter: Be still now!

Lindner: Well—

Ruth *(Still innocently)*: Would you like another chair—you don't look comfortable.

Lindner *(More frustrated than annoyed)*: No, thank you very much. Please. Well—to get right to the point I—*(A great breath, and he is off at last)* I am sure you people must be aware of some of the incidents which have happened in various parts of the city when colored people have moved into certain areas—*(Beneatha exhales heavily and starts tossing a piece of fruit up and down in the air)* Well—because we have what I think is going to be a unique type of organization in American community life—not only do we deplore that kind of thing—but we are trying to do something about it *(Beneatha stops tossing and turns with new and quizzical interest to the man)* We feel— *(gaining confidence in his mission because of the interest in the faces of the people he is talking to)* —we feel that most of the trouble in this world, when you come right down to it— *(He hits his knee for emphasis)* —most of the trouble exists because people just don't sit down and talk to each other.

Ruth (Nodding as she might in church, pleased with the remark): You can say that again, mister.

Lindner (More encouraged by such affirmation): That we don't try hard enough in this world to understand the other fellow's problem. The other guy's point of view.

Ruth: Now that's right.
(Beneatha and Walter merely watch and listen with genuine interest)

Lindner Yes—that's the way we feel out in Clybourne Park. And that's why I was elected to come here this afternoon and talk to you people. Friendly like, you know, the way people should talk to each other and see if we couldn't find some way to work this thing out. As I say, the whole business is a matter of *caring* about the other fellow. Anybody can see that you are a nice family of folks, hard working and honest I'm sure. *(Beneatha frowns slightly, quizzically, her head tilted regarding him)* Today everybody knows what it means to be on the outside of *something.* And of course, there is always somebody who is out to take the advantage of people who don't always understand.

Walter: What do you mean?

Lindner Well—you see, our community is made up of people who've worked hard as the dickens for years to build up that little community. They're not rich and fancy people; just hard-working, honest people who don't really have much but those little homes and a dream of the kind of community they want to raise their children in. Now, I don't say we are perfect and there is a lot wrong in some of the things they want. But you've got to admit that a man, right or wrong, has the right to want to have the neighborhood he lives in a certain kind of way. And at the moment the overwhelming majority of our people out there feel that people get along better, take more of a common interest in the life of the community, when they share a common background. I want you to believe me when I tell you that race prejudice simply doesn't enter into it. It is a matter of the people of Clybourne Park believing, rightly or wrongly, as I say, that for the happiness of all concerned that our Negro families are happier when they live in their *own* communities.

Beneatha: (With a grand and bitter gesture): This, friends, is the Welcoming Committee!

Walter (Dumfounded, looking at Lindner): Is this what you came marching all the way over here to tell us?

Lindner: Well, now we've been having a fine conversation. I hope you'll hear me all the way through.

Walter (Tightly): Go ahead, man.

Lindner: You see—in the face of all things I have said, we are prepared to make your family a very generous offer. . .

Beneatha: Thirty pieces and not a coin less!

Playwright and actress Lorraine Hansberry is best known for her play *A Raisin in the Sun.* With this work, she became both the youngest American to win the New York Drama Critics' Award and the first black woman to have a play on Broadway. *A Raisin in the Sun* was the first Broadway play directed by a black. Hansberry died of cancer in 1965. She was thirty-four years old.

Walter: Yeah?

Lindner (Putting on his glasses and drawing a form out of the briefcase): Our association is prepared, through the collective effort of our people, to buy the house from you at a financial gain to your family.

Ruth: Lord have mercy, ain't this the living gall!

Walter: All right, you through?

Lindner: Well, I want to give you the exact terms of the financial arrangement—

Walter: We don't want to hear no exact terms of no arrangements. I want to know if you got any more to tell us 'bout getting together?

Lindner (Taking off his glasses): Well—I don't suppose that you feel. . .

Walter: Never mind how I feel—you got any more to say 'bout how people ought to sit down and talk to each other? . . . Get out of my house, man.
(He turns his back and walks to the door)

Lindner (Looking around at the hostile faces and reaching and assembling his hat and briefcase): Well—I don't understand why you people are reacting this way. What do you think you are going to gain by moving into a neighborhood where you just aren't wanted and where some elements—well—people can get awful worked up when they feel that their whole way of life and everything they've ever worked for is threatened.

Walter: Get out.

Lindner (At the door, holding a small card): Well—I'm sorry it went like this.

Walter: Get out.

Lindner (Almost sadly regarding Walter): You just can't force people to change their hearts, son.
(He turns and puts his card on a table and exits. Walter pushes the door to with stinging hatred, and stands looking at it. Ruth just sits and Beneatha just stands. They say nothing. Mama and Travis enter)

Starting Time		Finishing Time	
Reading Time		Reading Rate	
Comprehension		Vocabulary	

Comprehension— Read the following questions and statements. For each one, put an *x* in the box before the option that contains the most complete or accurate answer. Check your answers in the Answer Key on page 107.

1. Mr. Lindner was initially looking for
   ☐ a. Mrs. Younger.   ☐ c. Walter.
   ☐ b. Mr. Younger.   ☐ d. Ruth.

2. The people of Clybourne Park were
   ☐ a. frugal.   ☐ c. prejudiced.
   ☐ b. religious.   ☐ d. thoughtful.

3. The situation in the passage can best be classified as
   ☐ a. fact and opinion.
   ☐ b. comparison and contrast.
   ☐ c. fiction and nonfiction.
   ☐ d. cause and effect.

4. The theme of Mr. Lindner's presentation is best expressed by which of the following pieces of dialogue?
   ☐ a. ". . . the whole business is a matter of caring about the other fellow."
   ☐ b. ". . . Negro families are happier when they live in their own communities."
   ☐ c. "Thirty pieces and not a coin less!"
   ☐ d. "You just can't force people to change their hearts, son."

5. Beneatha's suspicions are aroused when
   ☐ a. she opens the door.
   ☐ b. Lindner refuses all offers of hospitality.
   ☐ c. mention is made of the neighborhood council.
   ☐ d. Lindner leaves his calling card.

6. Two races are represented in this scene. One is portrayed as straightforward, the other as
   ☐ a. dignified.   ☐ c. reserved.
   ☐ b. insinuating.   ☐ d. hesitant.

7. "Thirty pieces and not a coin less!" is an allusion to
   ☐ a. the title of a Broadway musical.
   ☐ b. the betrayal of Christ by Judas.
   ☐ c. a private family joke.
   ☐ d. the price paid to the Indians for Manhattan.

8. For the Younger family, the expression "Welcoming Committee" is
   ☐ a. exaggerated.
   ☐ b. appropriate.
   ☐ c. ironic.
   ☐ d. inconsiderate.

9. Walter refuses to sell the Clybourne property at a profit because he
   ☐ a. is stubborn.
   ☐ b. lacks business sense.
   ☐ c. is pressured by his family.
   ☐ d. is a man of principle.

10. The author makes her point through
   ☐ a. dialogue.   ☐ c. figurative language.
   ☐ b. narrative.   ☐ d. parable.

Comprehension Skills

1. recalling specific facts	6. making a judgment
2. retaining concepts	7. making an inference
3. organizing facts	8. recognizing tone
4. understanding the main idea	9. understanding characters
5. drawing a conclusion	10. appreciation of literary forms

Study Skills, Part One—Following is a passage with blanks where words have been omitted. Next to the passage are groups of five words, one group for each blank. Complete the passage by circling the correct word for each of the blanks.

Terminal Signals

We have been looking at two types of signals that urge the reader on, words that indicate the continuance of the same thoughts and ideas.

You will recall that the second type of signal, the Summary Signal, indicates the appearance of an added or more ___(1)___ thought. That new thought, you have

(1)   serious   important
         developed   noteworthy   recent

learned, is brought about as a result or consequence of the previous ideas.

Yet another type of Forward Signal exists. The Terminal Signal, as it is known, plays a critical role in any written matter.

As the label suggests, Terminal Signals tell the reader that the author is ___(2)___ his remarks. They announce that he has developed all of the thoughts in his presentation, and that he is about to sum them up or ___(3)___ a conclusion. Some Terminal Signals are *as a result, finally,* and *in conclusion.* They tell the reader that an ongoing thought (which has been nurtured and developed with the aid of Forward Signals) is about to be terminated.

The main ___(4)___ between Summary and Terminal Signals is that sense of finality. Summary Signals indicate a pause in the forward motion of a thought. The writer uses the pause not only to sum up the original and the added ideas, but also to extend the ___(5)___ further. He has reached a summary point, but he is not yet ready to state the final conclusion.

Terminal Signals, on the other hand, end the account in an obvious way. Observe the following use of a Terminal Signal:

> Once the police patrols had been doubled
> and the aid of the occupants enlisted,
> the cat burglar was caught. *As a result,*
> this burglar's days of catting are all over.

The phrase *as a result* makes it plain that the author has said all he ___(6)___ to say on the subject.

As the textbook reader, you can well imagine that the Terminal Signal may present one of the ___(7)___ points of any chapter or lesson.

(2)	beginning		recording
	creating	concluding	designing

(3)		draw	invent
	guess	reverse	initiate

(4)	distinction		likeness
	connection	agreement	relationship

(5)	subject		division
	lesson	data	reaction

(6)	can		knows
	intends	permits	pretends

(7)	interesting		harmful
	major	minor	trivial

Study Skills, Part Two—Read the study skills passage again, paying special attention to the lesson being taught. Then, without looking back at the passage, complete each sentence below by writing in the missing word or words. Check the Answer Key on page 107 for the answers to Study Skills, Part One, and Study Skills, Part Two.

1. The last Forward Signals to be considered are the _____ Signals.

2. As the name suggests, these signals announce the _____ of the presentation.

3. The ideas following these last statements will be _____, not more of the same.

4. The main distinction between these signals and Summary Signals is the sense of _____ indicated by Terminal Signals.

5. These signals are important because they mark the completion of the writer's thoughts on the _____.

Funeral of a Whale

by J. Benibengor Blay

Vocabulary—The five words below are from the story you are about to read. Study the words and their meanings. Then complete the ten sentences that follow, using one of the five words to fill in the blank in each sentence. Mark your answer by writing the letter of the word on the line before the sentence. Check your answers in the Answer Key on page 107.

A. **strand:** the land bordering a body of water; the shore

B. **questing:** as one searching or in pursuit of something

C. **crane:** to stretch the neck, straining to see

D. **accord:** to grant or bestow upon

E. **anxious:** worried

_____ 1. The villagers became _____ as food supplies dwindled and starvation loomed.

_____ 2. The waves quietly advanced, broke upon the _____, and then retreated.

_____ 3. Even the gulls stopped their endless _____ for food to pay homage to the king.

_____ 4. All the villagers tried to _____ their necks to view the king of the sea.

_____ 5. At last everyone came together in one assembly to _____ a respectful homage to their king.

_____ 6. Made _____ by the troubled times, the natives prayed to the sea for help.

_____ 7. The whale's presence halted the fishermen in their slow, _____ progress along the shore.

_____ 8. Those standing in back of the gathered throng had to _____ their necks to see the chief.

_____ 9. It was the duty of each native to _____ a decent farewell to the whale.

_____ 10. Gallons of disinfectant had been sprinkled all along the _____ to kill the smell of rotting flesh.

There is great excitement in the ancient town of Missibi in Ghana.

The previous night had been wet and stormy and one which the fishermen were not likely to forget. Caught in the storm, their canoes had been dashed to pieces on the rocks and their nets swept away on the swift current. Only the fact that they were all strong swimmers had saved the men from drowning.

The sun is not yet up when they collect again on the shore to watch for their nets. The moon is still shining and little waves dance merrily on the strand, while the sea crabs scuttle among the scattered shells. But these things do not interest the fishermen, and even the search for nets is forgotten as they catch sight of a huge object, surrounded by a shoal of fish, tossing on the rolling sea. Their slow, questing advance is halted as a nauseating stench greets them. Fingers to their noses, they crane and peer. It is a whale—and judging by the smell, it has been dead for some days.

Now, such a sight is no mere spectacle to the people of Missibi. As descendents of a strong and virile race which long ago came by sea in great barge-like ships to settle in these parts, they hold to the tradition that the sea is their home and they worship it to this day. In any crisis—whatever its nature, whether drought or famine or war—they call upon the sea for help. The whale is the king of their sea. And it has been the custom, throughout their long history, to accord a ceremonial funeral to any whale that comes rolling ashore dead.

So, bound by tradition, the fishermen must bear the unhappy tidings to the ruler of the town. Their waists girdled with palm leaves and fingers to lips as signs that their news is urgent, and as yet secret, they go on their errand.

The chief's advisers are called together by the court messenger for a palaver. Now the fishermen are permitted to tell their news. Only after the chief's bodyguards have visited the beach to confirm this statement may the townsfolk be told. It is now past eight o'clock in the morning. The state drums boom out the warning of great calamity. The people from the busy market place, the farmers, coconut breakers and rice growers who have risen at cockcrow and gone to the farms, all come trooping to the palace yard, agog with excitement.

The chief comes to the courtyard with his advisers and sits on the landing of the dais. His face betokens sadness. His attendants bow and leave the palace. The drums are still booming. Outside are packed lorries and cars from up country bringing loads of hawkers and buyers to the market while the occupants move in with the still surging crowd.

The court messenger comes into the yard, bows to the chief and courtiers, commands silence and after giving a brief survey of the history of Missibi and her connection with the sea, makes his announcement to the assembled throng.

When the king of the sea dies, the people of Missibi go to the shore in mourning . . . and in celebration.

"The State is in mourning. A whale is dead and has been washed ashore. The funeral will be held at two o'clock at Aposika where the king of the sea now lies."

There is no whisper nor laughter nor cough as the great crowd moves from distant parts, out of the palace. The market day is postponed. The school bell's tolling stopped. All is sad silence. Yet it is a great day for the hawkers from distant parts, for now they will see something of which so far they have only heard. To the aged of the town it is history repeating itself, and the announcement seems to bring back pictures of half-forgotten times.

By order of a committee appointed by the chief's advisers, funeral preparations are put in hand at once. Cases of gin, beer, kola and palm wine are brought from the stores and cellars. A body of young men is engaged in the erection of bamboo huts, and the bush around the area is cleared, while musicians polish their instruments in readiness. Word is passed to neighboring places and more people arrive to swell the numbers.

At two o'clock the procession leaves for the scene of the funeral, guns booming, state guns rumbling, ivory horn blaring. The chief and his counselors are dressed in red. The womenfolk, besmeared with red clay and wearing pieces of red calico tied around their hair, are in front with the children. The men bring up the rear.

The tail of the column is as yet only at the outskirts of the town when its head reaches the place where a little off the beach, lies the great shapeless mass of the whale. Gallons of disinfectant have already been sprinkled around to kill the smell.

Now the chief's messenger calls for silence and orders the crowd to be seated. The chief steps forward followed by his advisers. Dropping the red cloth from his shoulder and gathering the folds in his left arm, with a glass of rum held in his right hand, he first raises his eyes to heaven then looks to the ground as he pours out a libation with these words: "Tradition binds us to the sea and the whale is king of the elements there. My people and I pay you homage and lament your death. How it happened we do not know. Whether it was in combat with your fellow kings, or whether it was inflicted by those who delight in making sport of you, or whether it was a natural death, we are afflicted all the same with a great sense of personal loss. We reaffirm our traditional ties with your descendents, will look to them in anxious days for help, and beg of you, who now belong to the ages, to release this land from starvation and sickness; leave in their place health and plenty. Rest in peace."

The funeral ceremony being declared open, the women like minstrels tell the story of the whale in parables; its connection with the state is recounted and the dead one praised. The chief and his advisers are head mourners and make themselves responsible for the fair distribution of drinks, providing food for those who have come from afar and recording donations received.

The young men keep order and play native instruments, while the old correct any departure from the traditional funeral procedure. Boys and girls play "Hunt the Slipper" and "Ampay." Hunters fire off guns and firecrackers at intervals in honor of the majesty of the dead. Fishermen fish in the waves and cast their nets on the beach; farmers sow their seeds on the strand, fetish priests play tom-toms and perform their feats of walking barefoot on broken bottles and gashing their stomachs with sharp knives. Everybody, in fact, is doing something. And all the men are partly or completely drunk.

As the celebration continues, weeping becomes the order of the day; there is competition among the womenfolk in pitch, tone and rendering of phrases, and prizes are offered to those who maintain the high standard of wailing set by their ancestors.

Further away from the crowds a great number of seagulls gather. Some are twittering, others are flying around the whale. The tide begins to rise and the waves are swelling high. Deep clouds overshadow the clear blue sky, and for a while the heavens are pouring rain. It seems that nature, too, is paying tribute to the king of the sea.

At six o'clock, as the sun is setting behind the clouds, the celebrations reach their climax—the solemn spreading of a long white sheet over the whale. Now each mourner takes a pebble, a shell, a stick, a coin or anything handy and, whispering a few words, whirls it around his head and throws it in the direction of the whale. Then without a further glance, all return to town.

The funeral of the king of the sea is over.

J. Benibengor Blay's short stories and poetry are popular in Ghana and other West African countries. He has written twenty-six books and pamphlets, numerous radio scripts, and many newspaper articles.

Blay has served as the Deputy Minister of Education and the Minister of Arts and Culture in the Government of the First Republic of Ghana. He has traveled extensively in Europe and America.

Starting Time		Finishing Time	
Reading Time		Reading Rate	
Comprehension		Vocabulary	

Comprehension — Read the following questions and statements. For each one, put an *x* in the box before the option that contains the most complete or accurate answer. Check your answers in the Answer Key on page 107.

1. The story takes place in
   □ a. Saudi Arabia.   □ c. Mexico.
   □ b. India.   □ d. Ghana.

2. The people of Missibi traced their ancestry to
   □ a. Egyptians.   □ c. Vikings.
   □ b. whales.   □ d. seafarers.

3. The events in the story take place
   □ a. over one month.
   □ b. over two weeks.
   □ c. over a week.
   □ d. within twenty-four hours.

4. The selection deals with
   □ a. current events.
   □ b. recorded history.
   □ c. traditional beliefs and rituals.
   □ d. ancient superstitions and myths.

5. The villagers do their fishing
   □ a. at night.
   □ b. at sunrise.
   □ c. at noontime.
   □ d. in the afternoon.

6. The serious and detailed preparations for the unusual funeral may seem, to an outsider,
   □ a. degrading.
   □ b. outrageous.
   □ c. remarkable.
   □ d. hilarious.

7. The color red symbolizes
   □ a. authority.
   □ b. mourning.
   □ c. festivity.
   □ d. jealousy.

8. The overall tone of the selection is
   ☐ a. suspenseful.
   ☐ b. somber.
   ☐ c. humorous.
   ☐ d. mysterious.

9. The people and the officials of Missibi are
   ☐ a. crude and common.
   ☐ b. pious and serious.
   ☐ c. sincere and natural.
   ☐ d. clever and calculating.

10. The words "in combat with your fellow kings" show the use of
    ☐ a. an exclamation.   ☐ c. euphemism.
    ☐ b. comparison.   ☐ d. personification.

Study Skills, Part One—Following is a passage with blanks where words have been omitted. Next to the passage are groups of five words, one group for each blank. Complete the passage by circling the correct word for each of the blanks.

Counter Signals

We have been looking mainly at Forward Signals, those signals that tell the reader that a thought is ___(1)___, that more of the same is coming. We have also discussed Terminal Signals, which are words and phrases the writer uses to tell the reader that an ongoing thought is about to come to an end.

The last signal we will examine does a different job; it signals a reversal of the thought. Called a Counter Signal, this device turns the thought sharply in a different ___(2)___. It tells the reader to be alert, because a countering idea is soon to appear.

Some common Counter Signals are *but, yet, nevertheless, otherwise, although, despite, in spite of, not, on the contrary,* and *however.* They are all used to introduce an idea not only ___(3)___ from what has gone before, but also one that leads the reader in a new direction.

By far the most common Counter Signal is *but.* In the words of English poet Samuel Daniel, "Oh, now comes that bitter word—*but,* which makes all nothing that was ___(4)___ before, that smooths and wounds, that strikes and dashes more than flat denial, or a plain disgrace."

Most of us, like Daniel, can testify to the power of the word. At one time or another we've all overlooked it and suffered the consequences. It is a little word, but it's packed with ___(5)___. Don't pass over it in your reading—check to see how it affects the sense of the passage.

Indeed, when you come upon any of the Counter Signals, prepare yourself. They tell you that the thought is not going ___(6)___ any longer, that it has stopped. And in textbooks especially, be alert for Counter Signals. They indicate that the author has come to a ___(7)___ in the road and is about to go in a different direction.

(1)   ending   beginning
       stopping   continuing   developing

(2)   direction   station
          form   line   group

(3)   adapted   remaining
       different   continuing   taken

(4)   removed   spent
       traded   separated   said

(5)   joy   significance
       expression   emotion   depression

(6)   forward   backward
       smoothly   slowly   quickly

(7)   man   place
       turn   sign   detour

Study Skills, Part Two—Read the study skills passage again, paying special attention to the lesson being taught. Then, without looking back at the passage, complete each sentence below by writing in the missing word or words. Check the Answer Key on page 107 for the answers to Study Skills, Part One, and Study Skills, Part Two.

1. The final signals to be considered are different from the Forward Signals. They are called _____ signals.

2. Counter Signals indicate a _____ in thought.

3. Counter Signals not only introduce a different idea, but they also _____ the reader in a new direction.

4. *But* is the most common and probably the most powerful of these words, because it can change the entire _____ of the passage.

5. When you come upon a Counter Signal in a textbook, _____ yourself for a change in direction.

The Interesting Narrative
of the Life of Gustavus Vassa

Vocabulary—The five words below are from the story you are about to read. Study the words and their meanings. Then complete the ten sentences that follow, using one of the five words to fill in the blank in each sentence. Mark your answer by writing the letter of the word on the line before the sentence. Check your answers in the Answer Key on page 107.

A. confirm: to strengthen one's belief

B. meanest: most wretched, lacking in social position and power

C. consternation: fright and confusion

D. suffered: permitted, allowed

E. quartered: kept in a lodging place; housed

_____ 1. Everything that took place served to _____ Vassa's fears that he would never again see his home.

_____ 2. The captives were so tightly _____ there was barely an inch to turn around.

_____ 3. Some of the slaves were _____ to enjoy a moment of fresh air on deck.

_____ 4. The _____ that initially filled Vassa's mind was not relieved in the days that followed.

_____ 5. It didn't take long to _____ that all the captives would be ill-treated.

_____ 6. The _____ conditions in Vassa's homeland were not as awful as the conditions on the ship.

_____ 7. Some of the weaker slaves _____ below deck died before they could again see the light of day.

_____ 8. A feeling of _____ was clearly to be seen on the faces of the captives.

_____ 9. After enduring several weeks of the _____ surroundings, many of the natives jumped overboard in desperation.

_____ 10. In time the natives would be _____ to leave the ship for the auction block.

The first object which saluted my eyes when I arrived on the coast was the sea, and a slave ship, which was then riding at anchor, and waiting for its cargo. These filled me with astonishment, which was soon connected with terror, when I was carried on board. I was immediately handled, and tossed up to see if I were sound, by some of the crew; and I was now persuaded that I had gotten into a world of bad spirits, and that they were going to kill me. Their complexions too differing so much from ours, their long hair, and the language they spoke (which was very different from any I had ever heard), united to confirm me in this belief.

Indeed, such were the horrors of my views and fears at the moment, that, if ten thousand worlds had been my own, I would have freely parted with them all to have exchanged my condition with that of the meanest slave in my own country. When I looked round the ship too and saw a large furnace of copper boiling, and a multitude of black people of every description chained together, every one of their countenances expressing dejection and sorrow, I no longer doubted of my fate; and, quite overpowered with horror and anguish, I fell motionless on the deck and fainted.

When I recovered a little, I found some black people about me, whom I believed were some of those who had brought me on board, and had been receiving their pay; they talked to me in order to cheer me, but all in vain. I asked them if I were not to be eaten by those white men with horrible looks, red faces, and long hair. They told me I was not; and one of the crew brought me a small portion of spirituous liquor in a wine glass; but being afraid of him, I would not take it out of his hand. One of the blacks therefore took it from him and gave it to me, and I took a little down my palate, which, instead of reviving me, as I thought it would, threw me into the greatest consternation at the strange feeling it produced, having never tasted any such liquor before.

Soon after this, the blacks who brought me on board went off, and left me abandoned to despair. I now saw myself deprived of all chance of returning to my native country, or even the least glimpse of hope of gaining the shore, which I now considered as friendly; and I even wished for my former slavery in preference to my present situation, which was filled with horrors of every kind, still heightened by my ignorance of what I was to undergo.

I was not long suffered to indulge my grief; I was soon put down under the decks, and there I received such a salutation in my nostrils as I had never experienced in my life: so that with the loathsomeness of the stench and crying together, I became so sick and low that I was not able to eat, nor had I the least desire to taste anything.

I now wished for the last friend, death, to relieve me; but soon, to my grief, two of the white men offered me eatables; and, on my refusing to eat, one of them held me fast by the hands, and laid me across, I think, the windlass,

Picture yourself thrown in chains, flogged if you are too sick to eat, tortured so you wish for death—and you are sailing toward a life of slavery.

and tied my feet, while the other flogged me severely.

I had never experienced anything of this kind before; and although, not being used to the water, I naturally feared that element the first time I saw it, yet nevertheless, could I have got over the nettings, I would have jumped over the side, but I could not; and, besides, the crew used to watch us very closely who were not chained down to the decks, lest we should leap into the water: and I have seen some of these poor African prisoners most severely cut for attempting to do so, and hourly whipped for not eating. This indeed was often the case with myself.

In a little time after, amongst the poor chained men, I found some of my own nation, which in a small degree gave ease to my mind. I inquired of these what was to be done with us. They gave me to understand we were to be carried to these white people's country to work for them. I then was a little revived, and thought, if it were no worse than working, my situation was not so desperate.

But still I feared I should be put to death, the white people looked and acted, as I thought, in so savage a manner; for I had never seen among any people such instances of brutal cruelty; and this not only shown towards us blacks, but also to some of the whites themselves.

One white man in particular I saw, when we were permitted on deck, flogged so unmercifully with a large rope near the foremast, that he died in consequence of it; and they have tossed him over the side as they would have done a brute. This made me fear these people the more; and I expected nothing less than to be treated in the same manner.

I could not help expressing my fears and apprehensions to some of my countrymen: I asked them if these people had no country, but lived in this hollow place (the ship). They told me they did not, but came from a distant one.

"Then," said I, "how comes it in all our country we 'never heard of them!' " They told me because they lived so very far off. I then asked where were their women. Had they any like themselves? I was told they had: "And why," said I, "do we not see them?" They answered, because they were left behind.

I asked how the vessel could go? They told me they could not tell; but that there were cloth put upon the masts by the help of the ropes I saw, and then the vessel went on; and the white men had some spell or magic they put in the water when they liked in order to stop the vessel. I was exceedingly amazed at this account, and really thought they were spirits. I therefore wished much to be from amongst them, for I expected they would sacrifice me: but my wishes were in vain; for we were so quartered that it was impossible for any of us to make our escape.

While we stayed on the coast I was mostly on deck; and one day, to my great astonishment, I saw one of these vessels coming in with the sails up. As soon as the whites saw it, they gave a great shout, at which we were amazed; and the more so as the vessel appeared larger by approaching nearer. At last she came to an anchor in my sight, and when the anchor was let go I and my countrymen who saw it were lost in astonishment to observe the vessel stop; and were now convinced it was done by magic.

Soon after this the other ship got her boats out, and they came on board of us, and the people of both ships seemed very glad to see each other. Several of the strangers also shook hands with us, black people, and made motions with their hands, signifying I suppose, we were to go to their country; but we did not understand them.

At last, when the ship we were in had got in all her cargo, they made ready with many fearful noises, and we were all put under deck, so that we could not see how they managed the vessel.

But this disappointment was the least of my sorrow. The stench of the hold while we were on the coast was so intolerably loathsome that it was dangerous to remain there for any time, and some of us had been permitted to stay on the deck for the fresh air; but now that the whole ship's cargo were confined together, it became absolutely pestilential.

The closeness of the place, and the heat of the climate, added to the number in the ship, which was so crowded that each had scarcely room to turn himself, almost suffocated us. This produced copious perspirations, so that the air soon became unfit for respiration, from a variety of loathsome smells, and brought on a sickness among the slaves, of which many died, thus falling victims to the improvident avarice, as I may call it, of their purchasers.

This wretched situation was again aggravated by the galling of the chains, now become insupportable; and the filth of the necessary tubs, into which the children often fell, and were almost suffocated. The shrieks of the women, and the groans of the dying, rendered the whole a scene of horror almost inconceivable.

Happily perhaps for myself I was soon reduced so low here that it was thought necessary to keep me almost always on deck; and from my extreme youth I was not put in fetters. In this situation I expected every hour to share the fate of my companions, some of whom were almost daily brought upon deck at the point of death, which I began to hope would soon put an end to my miseries. Often did I think many of the inhabitants of the deep much more happy than myself. I envied them the freedom they enjoyed, and as often wished I could change my condition for theirs.

Every circumstance I met with served only to render my state more painful, and heightened my apprehensions, and my opinion of the cruelty of the whites. One day they had taken a number of fishes; and when they had killed and satisfied themselves with as many as they thought fit, to our astonishment who were on the deck, rather than give any of them to us to eat, as we expected, they tossed the remaining fish into the sea again, although we begged and prayed for some as well as we could, but in vain. Some of my countrymen, being pressed by hunger, took an opportunity, when they thought no one saw them, of trying

In the late 18th and early 19th centuries, an increasing number of blacks were taught to read and write, often by Christian owners who wanted them to understand the Bible. But many blacks used their knowledge to write about their own experiences as slaves, and the quality of their writing combined with the shocking subject matter made their narratives quite popular.

The most famous of such narratives was published by Olaudah Equiano, a former American slave, in London in 1789. Called *The Interesting Narrative of the Life of Gustavus Vassa, the African,* the book was widely read and reached its eighth edition in London only five years after publication. There were eventually ten editions of the book, not counting translations.

to get a little privately; but they were discovered, and the attempt procured them some very severe floggings.

One day, when we had a smooth sea and moderate wind, two of my wearied countrymen who were chained together (I was near them at the time), preferring death to such a life of misery, somehow made through the nettings and jumped into the sea: immediately another quite dejected fellow, who on account of his illness was suffered to be out of irons, also followed their example; and I believe many more would very soon have done the same if they had not been prevented by the ship's crew who were instantly alarmed.

Those of us that were the most active were in a moment put down under the deck, and there was such a noise and confusion amongst the people of the ship as I never heard before, to stop her, and get the boat out to go after the slaves. However, two of the wretches were drowned, but they got the other, and afterwards flogged him unmercifully for thus attempting to prefer death to slavery.

In this manner we continued to undergo more hardships than I can now relate, hardships which are inseparable from this accursed trade. Many a time we were near suffocation from the want of fresh air, which we were often without for whole days together. This, and the stench of the necessary tubs, carried off many.

At last we came in sight of the island of Barbados, at which the whites on board gave a great shout, and made many signs of joy to us. We did not know what to think of this; but as the vessel drew nearer we plainly saw the harbour, and other ships of different kinds and sizes; and we soon anchored amongst them off Bridge-Town.

Many merchants and planters now came on board, though it was in the evening. They put us in separate parcels, and examined us attentively. They also made us jump, and pointed to the land, signifying we were to go there. We thought by this we should be eaten by these ugly men, as they appeared to us; and, when soon after we were all put down under the deck again, there was much dread and trembling.

Starting Time		Finishing Time	
Reading Time		Reading Rate	
Comprehension		Vocabulary	

Comprehension— Read the following questions and statements. For each one, put an *x* in the box before the option that contains the most complete or accurate answer. Check your answers in the Answer Key on page 107.

1. The slave ship was headed for
   □ a. Jamestown.   □ c. the Cape Verde Islands.
   □ b. Barbados.   □ d. the New World.

2. Stripped of their dignity and reduced to a subhuman level, the captives
   □ a. fought among themselves.
   □ b. defied their guards.
   □ c. sought release in death.
   □ d. surrendered to the inevitable.

3. This story concerns Vassa's
   □ a. family.   □ c. childhood.
   □ b. education.   □ d. profession.

4. The theme of this selection can best be expressed by which of the following?
   □ a. Man's inhumanity to man makes countless thousands mourn.
   □ b. History repeats itself.
   □ c. Money is the source of all evil.
   □ d. Do unto others before they do unto you.

5. The one factor which made life aboard ship particularly intolerable was the
   □ a. ship's crew.
   □ b. congestion.
   □ c. practice of flogging.
   □ d. use of necessary tubs.

6. The wild fear that spread among the captives after the Bridge-Town merchants examined them resulted from
   □ a. past treatment and new surroundings.
   □ b. the cannibalistic reputation of the merchants.
   □ c. heated arguments between the merchants and the captors.
   □ d. sordid stories they had heard from other slaves.

7. Vassa's homeland was
   □ a. in the interior.
   □ b. on the coast.
   □ c. in Barbados.
   □ d. in North Africa.

8. The author's initial reaction was one of
   □ a. doubt.
   □ b. terror.
   □ c. anticipation.
   □ d. intimidation.

9. By analyzing the cruelty of the white men, Vassa shows us that he is
   □ a. physically fit.
   □ b. too sensitive.
   □ c. prone to exaggeration.
   □ d. perceptive.

10. The selection is written in the form of
   □ a. an essay.
   □ b. a narrative.
   □ c. a description.
   □ d. a diary.

Comprehension Skills

1. recalling specific facts	6. making a judgment
2. retaining concepts	7. making an inference
3. organizing facts	8. recognizing tone
4. understanding the main idea	9. understanding characters
5. drawing a conclusion	10. appreciation of literary forms

Study Skills, Part One—Following is a passage with blanks where words have been omitted. Next to the passage are groups of five words, one group for each blank. Complete the passage by circling the correct word for each of the blanks.

Mastering the Text, I

According to the old saying, a workman is only as good as his tools. That is, of course, if he knows how to use them. But what about students? Their tools of learning are textbooks, and the quality of their work depends in large measure on how ___(1)___ they use them.

(1)   poorly   well
         quickly   often   generously

Fortunately, most modern textbooks are well organized. Publishers try to be sure that their texts are up-to-date, broad in scope, and direct. Because texts are so well ___(2)___ , students can take advantage of those very features.

EVALUATE THE AUTHOR

Naturally, the author knows more about the ___(3)___ than you do; you cannot judge him on that basis. But you can try to learn about his background and experience. Is he a lecturer or professor? If so, where does he teach? In addition to teaching, does the writer work in the field? That information may tell you whether his ___(4)___ is theoretical or practical. The level at which he teaches may tell you how general or detailed his writing will be.

In looking for such background information, it is helpful to read the author's preface or introduction. There you will learn if he regards his text as an intensive discussion or a broad survey. You may also find out if he plans to draw on his experiences in the field. Most importantly, you can avail yourself of the chance to examine the author's ___(5)___ for writing the book. You will learn what is expected of you, and why the author considers the subject useful and necessary. Any ideas for you to keep in mind as you use the text should be covered in the preface. Such ___(6)___ remarks are designed to get you off to a good start.

In addition, you should check the copyright date to make sure that the book is current. In today's world, new ___(7)___ accumulates hourly. Therefore it is essential that textbook material is timely enough to be of use.

(2)		known	used
	oiled	constructed	appreciated

(3)		subject	history
	sincerity	intentions	associations

(4)		background	approach
	emotion	politics	contacts

(5)		salary	reason
	equipment	talent	preparation

(6)		closing	exciting
	opening	interesting	formal

(7)		study	information
	machinery	chemistry	experimentation

Study Skills, Part Two—Read the study skills passage again, paying special attention to the lesson being taught. Then, without looking back at the passage, complete each sentence below by writing in the missing word or words. Check the Answer Key on page 107 for the answers to Study Skills, Part One, and Study Skills, Part Two.

1. A good mechanic must know how to _____ his tools.

2. Publishers make an effort to produce _____ textbooks.

3. It is possible for the student to _____ about the author's background and experience.

4. Working in the field gives the author a _____ approach to the subject.

5. The first opportunity for the author to address the reader is offered by the _____ .

The Color Purple

by Alice Walker

Vocabulary—The five words below are from the story you are about to read. Study the words and their meanings. Then complete the ten sentences that follow, using one of the five words to fill in the blank in each sentence. Mark your answer by writing the letter of the word on the line before the sentence. Check your answers in the Answer Key on page 108.

A. harass: to bother someone to the point of becoming annoying

B. budge: to move from a position

C. vain: conceited

D. adrift: not certain, confused

E. conjure: think about, form a mental picture

_____ 1. No one could _____ Shug from her view of God.

_____ 2. Shug's idea of God was so confusing to Celie that it set her mind _____.

_____ 3. Some people like to _____ others with their religious views.

_____ 4. People who think they are wonderful are _____.

_____ 5. Celie was so engrossed in what Shug was saying she did not _____ from her chair.

_____ 6. It's not always easy to _____ up a picture of God.

_____ 7. According to Shug, God is not _____.

_____ 8. It's not nice to _____ people, even if you don't like them.

_____ 9. According to Shug, whenever you pray you should _____ up things you appreciate.

_____ 10. It is upsetting when conflicting emotions make you feel set _____.

Dear Nettie,

I don't write to God no more, I write to you.

What happen to God? ast Shug.

Who that? I say.

She look at me serious.

Big a devil as you is, I say, you not worried bout no God, surely.

She say, Wait a minute. Hold on just a minute here. Just because I don't harass it like some peoples us know don't mean I ain't got religion.

What God do for me? I ast.

She say, Celie! Like she shock. He gave you life, good health, and a good woman that love you to death.

Yeah, I say, and he give me a lynched daddy, a crazy mama, a lowdown dog of a step pa and a sister I probably won't ever see again. Anyhow, I say, the God I been praying and writing to is a man. And act just like all the other mens I know. Trifling, forgitful and lowdown.

She say, Miss Celie, You better hush. God might hear you.

Let 'im hear me, I say. If he ever listened to poor colored women the world would be a different place, I can tell you.

She talk and she talk, trying to budge me way from blasphemy. But I blaspheme much as I want to.

All my life I never care what people thought bout nothing I did, I say. But deep in my heart I care about God. What he going to think. And come to find out, he don't think. Just sit up there glorying in being deef, I reckon. But it ain't easy, trying to do without God. Even if you know he ain't there, trying to do without him is a strain.

I is a sinner, say Shug. Cause I was born. I don't deny it. But once you find out what's out there waiting for us, what else can you be?

Sinners have more good times, I say.

You know why? she ast.

Cause you ain't all the time worrying bout God, I say.

Naw, that ain't it, she say. Us worry bout God a lot. But once us feel loved by God, us do the best us can to please him with what us like.

You telling me God love you, and you ain't never done nothing for him? I mean, not go to church, sing in the choir, feed the preacher and all like that?

But if God love me, Celie, I don't have to do all that. Unless I want to. There's a lot of other things I can do that I speck God likes.

Like what? I ast.

Oh, she say. I can lay back and just admire stuff. Be happy. Have a good time.

Well, this sound like blasphemy sure nuff.

She say, Celie, tell the truth, have you ever found God in church? I never did. I just found a bunch of folks hoping for him to show. Any God I ever felt in church I brought in with me. And I think all the other folks

The gospel according to Shug, in which God is not a white, robed, barefoot, bearded man of indeterminate age.

did too. They come to church to *share* God, not find God.

Some folks didn't have him to share, I said. They the ones didn't speak to me while I was there struggling with my big belly and Mr. ____ children.

Right, she say.

Then she say: Tell me what your God look like, Celie.

Aw naw, I say. I'm too shame. Nobody ever ast me this before, so I'm sort of took by surprise. Besides, when I think about it, it don't seem quite right. But it all I got. I decide to stick up for him, just to see what Shug say.

Okay, I say. He big and old and tall and graybearded and white. He wear white robes and go barefooted.

Blue eyes? she ast.

Sort of bluish-gray. Cool. Big though. White lashes, I say.

She laugh.

Why you laugh? I ast. I don't think it so funny. What you expect him to look like, Mr. ____?

That wouldn't be no improvement, she say. Then she tell me this old white man is the same God she used to see when she prayed. If you wait to find God in church, Celie, she say, that's who is bound to show up, cause that's where he live.

How come? I ast.

Cause that's the one that's in the white folks' white bible.

Shug! I say. God wrote the bible, white folks had nothing to do with it.

How come he look just like them, then? she say. Only bigger? And a heap more hair. How come the bible just like everything else they make, all about them doing one thing and another, and all the colored folks doing is gitting cursed?

I never thought bout that.

Nettie say somewhere in the bible it say Jesus' hair was like lamb's wool, I say.

Well, say Shug, if he came to any of these churches we talking bout he'd have to have it conked before anybody paid him any attention. The last thing niggers want to think about they God is that his hair kinky.

That's the truth, I say.

Ain't no way to read the bible and not think God white, she say. Then she sigh. When I found out I thought God was white, and a man, I lost interest. You mad cause he don't seem to listen to your prayers. Humph! Do the mayor listen to anything colored say? Ask Sofia, she say.

But I don't have to ast Sofia. I know white people never listen to colored, period. If they do, they only listen long enough to be able to tell you what to do.

Here's the thing, say Shug. The thing I believe. God is inside you and inside everybody else. You come into the world with God. But only them that search for it inside find it. And sometimes it just manifest itself even if you not looking, or don't know what you looking for. Trouble do it for most folks, I think. Sorrow, lord. Feeling like shit.

It? I ast.

Yeah, It. God ain't a he or a she, but a It.

But what do it look like? I ast.

Don't look like nothing, she say. It ain't a picture show. It ain't something you can look at apart from anything else, including yourself. I believe God is everything, say Shug. Everything that is or ever was or ever will be. And when you can feel that, and be happy to feel that, you've found It.

Shug a beautiful something, let me tell you. She frown a little, look out cross the yard, lean back in her chair, look like a big rose.

She say, My first step from the old white man was trees. Then air. Then birds. Then other people. But one day when I was sitting quiet and feeling like a motherless child, which I was, it come to me: that feeling of being part of everything, not separate at all. I knew that if I cut a tree, my arm would bleed. And I laughed and I cried and I run all around the house. I knew just what it was. In fact, when it happen, you can't miss it. It sort of like you know what, she say, grinning and rubbing high up on my thigh.

Shug! I say.

Oh, she say. God love all them feelings. That's some of the best stuff God did. And when you know God loves 'em you enjoys 'em a lot more. You can just relax, go with everything that's going, and praise God by liking what you like.

God don't think it dirty? I ast.

Naw, she say. God made it. Listen, God love everything you love—and a mess of stuff you don't. But more than anything else, God love admiration.

You saying God vain? I ast.

Naw, she say. Not vain, just wanting to share a good thing. I think it pisses God off if you walk by the color purple in a field somewhere and don't notice it.

What it do when it pissed off? I ast.

Oh, it make something else. People think pleasing God is all God care about. But any fool living in the world can see it always trying to please us back.

Yeah? I say.

Yeah, she say. It always making little surprises and springing them on us when us least expect.

You mean it want to be loved, just like the bible say.

Yes, Celie, she say. Everything want to be loved. Us sing and dance, make faces and give flower bouquets, trying to be loved. You ever notice that trees do everything to git attention we do, except walk?

Well, us talk and talk bout God, but I'm still adrift. Trying to chase that old white man out of my head. I been so busy thinking bout him I never truly notice nothing God make. Not a blade of corn (how it do that?) not the color purple (where it come from?). Not the little wildflowers. Nothing.

Now that my eyes opening, I feels like a fool. Next to any little scrub of a bush in my yard, Mr. ____'s evil sort of shrink. But not altogether. Still, it is like Shug say, You have to git man off your eyeball, before you can see anything a'tall.

Man corrupt everything, say Shug. He on your box of grits, in your head, and all over the radio. He try to make you think he everywhere. Soon as you think he everywhere, you think he God. But he ain't. Whenever you trying to pray, and man plop himself on the other end of it, tell him to git lost, say Shug. Conjure up flowers, wind, water, a big rock.

But this hard work, let me tell you. He been there so long, he don't want to budge. He threaten lightening, floods and earthquakes. Us fight. I hardly pray at all. Every time I conjure up a rock, I throw it.

Best known for her highly acclaimed third novel *The Color Purple,* Alice Walker has also written volumes of short stories and poems. Themes of racism and sexism are predominant in Walker's work and her central characters are generally black women.

Walker received the Pulitzer Prize and the American Book Award in 1983 for *The Color Purple.* She received the Guggenheim Award in 1977, was nominated for the National Book Critics Circle Award in 1982, and has received various writing fellowships. Walker resides in San Francisco, California.

Starting Time	*Finishing Time*
Reading Time	*Reading Rate*
Comprehension	*Vocabulary*

Comprehension— Read the following questions and statements. For each one, put an *x* in the box before the option that contains the most complete or accurate answer. Check your answers in the Answer Key on page 108.

1. Who is writing this letter?
   - ☐ a. Nettie
   - ☐ b. Shug
   - ☐ c. Celie
   - ☐ d. Sofia

2. It can be said of Shug that she
   - ☐ a. does not fear God.
   - ☐ b. is a terrible sinner.
   - ☐ c. will not seek redemption.
   - ☐ d. is a strict Catholic.

3. The ideas of Shug and Celie are presented in the form of
   - ☐ a. time order.
   - ☐ b. a spatial relationship.
   - ☐ c. contrasting views.
   - ☐ d. a simple list.

4. The main point of the selection can best be stated in which of the following?
   - ☐ a. God is fearful.
   - ☐ b. God can be angry.
   - ☐ c. God is the Church.
   - ☐ d. God loves admiration.

5. The passage hints that Celie
   - ☐ a. does not believe in God.
   - ☐ b. is angry at God.
   - ☐ c. takes God for granted.
   - ☐ d. works for the church.

6. Celie is more apt to listen to Shug because
   - ☐ a. Shug is much older than Celie.
   - ☐ b. the two women are friends.
   - ☐ c. they live together.
   - ☐ d. Celie does not have a mind of her own.

7. Shug implies that God is a
   - ☐ a. mere statue.
   - ☐ b. type of inner feeling.
   - ☐ c. flesh-and-blood being.
   - ☐ d. ghostlike being.

8. The overall tone of this selection is
   - ☐ a. depressing and morbid.
   - ☐ b. witty.
   - ☐ c. a mixture of sarcastic, reverent, and preachy.
   - ☐ d. a combination of serious and humorous.

9. As far as her beliefs go, Shug is
   - ☐ a. happy and content.
   - ☐ b. hardworking and frugal.
   - ☐ c. frustrated and depressed.
   - ☐ d. bored and angry.

10. The writer develops the selection through the use of
   - ☐ a. facts and statistics.
   - ☐ b. examples.
   - ☐ c. questions and answers.
   - ☐ d. metaphors.

Comprehension Skills

1. recalling specific facts	6. making a judgment
2. retaining concepts	7. making an inference
3. organizing facts	8. recognizing tone
4. understanding the main idea	9. understanding characters
5. drawing a conclusion	10. appreciation of literary forms

Study Skills, Part One—Following is a passage with blanks where words have been omitted. Next to the passage are groups of five words, one group for each blank. Complete the passage by circling the correct word for each of the blanks.

Mastering the Text, II

After checking on the author, it will be of help to look at two of the standard features of a textbook, the Table of Contents and the Bibliography.

Table of Contents. Next to the chapters themselves, this is the most important part of the ___(1)___ . It shows not only the material covered, but also how the material is

(1)   text   lesson
chapter   bibliography   features

organized. If the subject is dealt with historically, from its beginnings to the present, you know that the most current material will come at the end.

The author's approach may not be historical. For instance, if it is an analytic approach, the simple, basic ideas will be discussed ___(2)___ in the text. You will need to know and understand those if you are to grasp complex material presented later.

In examining the table of contents you can tell how the subject will be ___(3)___, even if you are not well versed in it. You may see listed in the table of contents a section that interests you. Prereading that section will add to your ___(4)___ in the subject area and may help you appreciate the rest of the material in the text.

The Bibliography. At the end of a book you will find the bibliography, which is a list of other books that were used by the author as ___(5)___ or source materials. That list can be a good indication of how the author put the book together. For instance, by reading the publishing dates of the books listed, you can see if the author used both early and ___(6)___ books on the subject. By examining the level of the sources you can judge if they are comprehensive or highly specialized. Perhaps you will even see a book cited that you will want to read for ___(7)___ information.

(2)
late   thoroughly
early   briefly   thoughtfully

(3)
determined   learned
understood   presented   decided

(4)
assistance   background
situation   character   analysis

(5)
reference   dictionary
glossary   aids   biography

(6)
historical   current
fiction   famous   unauthorized

(7)
additional   interesting
assigned   neglected   basic

Study Skills, Part Two—Read the study skills passage again, paying special attention to the lesson being taught. Then, without looking back at the passage, complete each sentence below by writing in the missing word or words. Check the Answer Key on page 108 for the answers to Study Skills, Part One, and Study Skills, Part Two.

1. The table of contents reveals the material covered in the book and how it

   is _____.

2. _____ presentation proceeds from the earliest to the latest.

3. Analytical presentation proceeds from the simple to the _____.

4. After looking at the table of contents, you may wish to _____

   a section that sounds interesting.

5. The bibliography is a list of books used by the author to obtain

   _____ on his subject.

Reggie

*by Reggie Jackson
with Mike Lupica*

Vocabulary—The five words below are from the story you are about to read. Study the words and their meanings. Then complete the ten sentences that follow, using one of the five words to fill in the blank in each sentence. Mark your answer by writing the letter of the word on the line before the sentence. Check your answers in the Answer Key on page 108.

A. ludicrous: ridiculous

B. catalyst: something that causes change, but remains unchanged itself

C. commentator: one who describes or comments on events

D. hectic: exciting and busy

E. feisty: having a fiery personality

_____ 1. Reggie had been such a good hitter that his .173 average seemed _____ .

_____ 2. The dugout got _____ when old Yankee friends came over to visit Reggie.

_____ 3. Not too many players were _____ enough to stand up to Steinbrenner.

_____ 4. Reggie wanted to prove that it was _____ of Steinbrenner to think that Reggie's career was at an end.

_____ 5. The chanting crowd was the _____ Reggie needed to spur his determination.

_____ 6. Working as a sports _____ was a job some baseball players did during the off-season.

_____ 7. Guidry's remark acted as a _____ in arousing Reggie's anger.

_____ 8. The catcher's _____ character was revealed by his spirited remarks.

_____ 9. It was more fun playing ball than being a _____ and having to tell about it.

_____ 10. Popular sports figures often lead a _____ life.

Now it was April 1982. I had signed with the Angels as a free agent after George Steinbrenner didn't think I could play anymore. I was happy to be back home in California. I always wanted to wind up my career in California. But after the first month or so of the season, I was making Steinbrenner look pretty smart. I was hitting .173 when I came into Yankee Stadium. I had no home runs. On the plane to New York, I sat next to Rick Burleson, our shortstop and a hell of a player. I once told Rick that I would like to think of myself as the type of player I think he is—an all-out, hard-nosed SOB. Anyway, on the plane, I was joking around with Burleson. I told him that I was really glad finally to be playing on the same team with him after all those years when he was with the Red Sox and I was with the Yankees. Burleson asked why.

I said, " 'Cause you're the only player on this team with a lower batting average than mine." Burleson was hitting a cool .161 at the time.

It had been an April of cap pistols and pea shooters.

I was coming back to the Stadium. For five years, we had put on the greatest baseball show on earth there. Perhaps the greatest sports show, period. There had been two world championships, three pennants, four divisional titles. Some of it had been good, some of it had been bad, a lot of it had been just plain ludicrous. There had never been a show quite like it, and I had been the catalyst somehow, the lightning rod, the center of the storms. Now I was coming back, and one more time I had a lot to prove. To my ex-teammates, who'd be looking at me from the dugout across the way. To the Yankee fans in the stands. To the owner up in his private box. To my own teammates, who were probably starting to wonder what this Reggie fuss was all about.

Mostly to myself. It had always been this way, no matter what I've done and where I've gone. One more battle. One more war. One more swing. Can he still do it? Can Reggie still produce? Funny thing—I was asking myself those very same questions. I figured that if I couldn't hit one out in this type of situation—a Reggie Situation if there ever was one—then maybe I couldn't do it anymore.

I had been pointing to April 27 for a long time, practically since I signed with the Angels. In February, I was working as a commentator for ABC Sports on their "Superstars" show in Key Biscayne, Florida. A writer from New York, Phil Pepe of the *Daily News*, came down and asked me if I'd thought about my first time back to New York as an Angel.

I said, "Not really." But I had. I'd been playing it down, not saying very much about it. But I'd thought about it a great deal. In a way, my season was going to be starting there, one way or another. For better or worse. Richer or poorer. And I really was ambivalent. My emotions were all mixed up. I didn't know whether to be scared or happy

Then from five thousand throats
and more there rose a lusty yell;
It rumbled through the valley,
it rattled in the dell;
It knocked upon the mountain
and recoiled upon the flat,
For Reggie, mighty Reggie,
was advancing to the bat.
—adapted from "Casey at the Bat" by E.L. Thayer

or joyous or uncomfortable. I had left on a bad note. We'd lost the World Series to the Dodgers. Steinbrenner said I couldn't play, that I'd asked him for a long-term contract and he couldn't commit to one because I was getting old. I was supposed to be a negative.

A cancer.

I always thought his views about my contract demands were sort of amusing since we never had one contract talk in all the months leading up to my free agency, or even after that. He would say he offered me three years and I asked for four. Well, he never made me an offer of any kind, so I had nothing at all against which to make a counteroffer. Maybe he is a mind reader.

So I wanted to go back and play against the Yankees, and I didn't want to. As we got closer and closer to the trip East, that was all anyone wanted to ask me about. Have you thought about going back? What do you think it will be like? I kept playing it down. But you're damn right I was thinking about it. And trying to be like Cool Hand Luke. Getting my mind right. Because on top of everything else, Ron Guidry was going to be pitching against us.

I'd always been proud to play with Guidry. I've called him the truest Yankee, because he was one of the few who had come all the way up through their system and seemed to *belong* in pinstripes. Guidry never bitched. He always just said, "Gimme the ball." Now he was on the other side. He'd come after me with left-handed sliders and fastballs, and I wanted to take him deep.

I thought: It would have to be Guidry.

The afternoon before the game was hectic. Two press conferences. One was for the Pony shoe company. There was another one later at the Stadium to make it easier for the writers since everyone was going to want to talk to me. I didn't mind doing the press conferences. I could always deal with the press. But throughout the whole day, what I mostly was was afraid. I was at .173. I was struggling. I wasn't Reggie. Those were the thoughts I couldn't get out of my mind.

I finally got out to the Stadium about two o'clock in the afternoon and hit for about forty-five minutes. In the middle of it, I started to feel decent. Not great. Decent. I was going to be in the other clubhouse and the other dugout, but I was in a familiar ballpark. It will always be The House That Ruth Built, but I had my times there. Ruth may have built it, but I managed to put some jazz in there. I began to hit some shots into the right-center-field bleachers. Then I hit some into the black—the seats they don't sell, the ones in dead center that they paint black to give the hitter a better background. I felt comfortable. Bobby Knoop, one of our coaches, was pitching to me. Unfortunately, I was aware that hitting against Bobby Knoop was not hitting against Ron Guidry.

Gene Mauch was our manager. Gene liked to play all

right-handed hitters against Guidry. He played things by the book, too much sometimes. But he came over to me after I finished hitting and just said, "I know you have to be in there tonight."

I said, "Gene, I don't have any business in the world being in there tonight against Guidry the way I've been going. But, yeah, I got to be there."

After that afternoon practice it was idle time. I was sitting in the clubhouse around three-thirty, basically alone. The players don't have to arrive until five-thirty or six for a night game. While I was sitting and thinking—mostly about Guidry—Maury Allen, a writer from the *New York Post*, came by for a chat. Allen said, "Reggie, I was just over in the Yankee clubhouse. Everybody is talking about what it's like for you to be back in Yankee Stadium, what it's going to be like for the Yankees to be facing you."

I told him that was natural, considering the history of everything.

Then Allen told me he'd asked Guidry about facing me and that Guidry had said, "Go ask Reggie what it's going to be like facing *me*."

I took that comment to be a bit condescending. Granted, I was defensive, probably looking for something to give me an extra edge. So I felt a little slighted because I'd always been such a Guidry fan. I consider him a friend to this day. Later on, I was sure Allen misrepresented Guidry a little because after the game, after I'd done what I did, Guidry got into trouble with Steinbrenner for saying, "It was the only fun I had all night." But I was glad Allen came by. I was able to get mad at Guidry for a couple of hours.

When I got back onto the field for batting practice, I still felt good at the plate. I hit more balls into the seats and got a nice reaction from the crowd that had showed up early, and the media and my old teammates. I needed that support. I was still insecure—I couldn't get .173 out of my mind—but I was starting to relax. Willie Randolph, the tough little second baseman who I feel Steinbrenner turned sullen because he never showed him enough appreciation, came over and shook my hand.

One of the most famous sluggers in modern baseball history, Reggie Jackson achieved early success with the Oakland Athletics, hitting 254 home runs for the team and helping them win three consecutive world championships during the early 1970s. He twice led the American League in home runs and hitting and was declared the league's Most Valuable Player in 1973. Jackson spent one season with the Baltimore Orioles before signing a contract with the New York Yankees in 1977.

Despite disputes with teammates, the owner, and the manager, Jackson played well for the Yankees, leading the team to a world championship in 1977 with three consecutive home runs in the final game. Following a disappointing season in 1981, Jackson joined the California Angels. Jackson has written extensively about baseball in books such as *Inside Hitting, Reggie: A Season with a Superstar,* and his autobiography, *Reggie.*

And Dave Winfield, the Twenty-five Million Dollar Man—a big man, big smile—Steinbrenner's stud apparent, who was supposed to take my place but wouldn't, couldn't ever quite take my place. He was, however, carving out Dave Winfield's place. And Rick Cerone, the feisty catcher. How feisty? He told George to fuck off to his face one time. Is that feisty enough for you? And Tommy John came by, a friend who'd been a classy Christian gentleman every day of his career. I was on the wrong side of the field, but they seemed glad to see me. Which is the way it should have been. We'd been through wars together. In a way it was like a little reunion.

Right before the game, I was running in the outfield, and Guidry came out of the bullpen like he always does, walking slowly, his left arm in his jacket. I thought, "Uh-oh. Here comes that SOB with his slider and his fastball, and I ain't got my guns loaded."

When I came to the plate the first time, there was a lot of noise, the old symphony of cheers and applause and some boos. But most of it was warm. Suddenly they were chanting, "REG-gie! REG-gie," just like always. I heard it, and I felt glad that they remembered, but all I was thinking was, "How am I going to hit this man's slider?"

He threw me a slider that first time up, and I popped out. Still I felt I made a pretty good pass at it. I got back to the dugout, and Gene Mauch said, "You just missed that one, you know." I knew I had a good pass. Next time up I pulled off a little bit, but managed to get a single up the middle. As I stood there on first base, I could feel the blood pumping. I was off and running.

I walked after that. By the time I got up in the seventh, It was drizzling steadily. The score was 2-1 in our favor. I felt ready. I was comfortable, and the fans were making me feel more welcome every time I came to the plate. I could feel them rooting for me. Rooting for a dinger. Guidry hung a slider and I just exploded all over it. I mean, it was *kissed.* The ball ended up hitting the facing of the upper deck and damn near bounced back to Randolph at second base. As I rounded the bases, I remember watching Ken Griffey picking the ball up in short right and throwing it back in. The Stadium went crazy. I felt like a dam at Niagara Falls had burst—for me, for the fans, even for the Yankees. I knew the Yankees felt good for me. They had seen me do it before. Now they were seeing me do it at a time when they knew I needed to do it.

Now the chant really went up.

"REG-gie! REG-gie!"

This was a sound, a stadium, I knew. I had been here before.

Starting Time		Finishing Time	
Reading Time		Reading Rate	
Comprehension		Vocabulary	

Comprehension— Read the following questions and statements. For each one, put an *x* in the box before the option that contains the most complete or accurate answer. Check your answers in the Answer Key on page 108.

1. In which year did Reggie sign with the Angels?
   - ☐ a. 1980
   - ☐ b. 1981
   - ☐ c. 1982
   - ☐ d. 1983

2. At the beginning of the selection, Reggie's career as a baseball player
   - ☐ a. had ended.
   - ☐ b. was in a slump.
   - ☐ c. was up and coming.
   - ☐ d. showed promise.

3. Reggie recounts his three times at bat in
   - ☐ a. numerical order.
   - ☐ b. spatial order.
   - ☐ c. chronological order.
   - ☐ d. a list.

4. Choose the best title for this selection from those given below.
   - ☐ a. Life at Yankee Stadium
   - ☐ b. Black Sports Figures
   - ☐ c. Superstars Galore
   - ☐ d. A Great Comeback

5. This passage hints that Ron Guidry was
   - ☐ a. Reggie's worst enemy.
   - ☐ b. well educated.
   - ☐ c. an abrasive character.
   - ☐ d. a good pitcher.

6. From the facts presented in the selection, we can make the judgment that Reggie was
   - ☐ a. well liked by many fans.
   - ☐ b. an embarrassment to his team.
   - ☐ c. afraid of flying.
   - ☐ d. once a good friend of Steinbrenner.

7. From the events described we can tell that Reggie was known mainly as a
   - ☐ a. good fielder.
   - ☐ b. commentator.
   - ☐ c. power hitter.
   - ☐ d. good friend of George Steinbrenner's.

8. In the last part of the selection, Reggie sounds as if he feels
   - ☐ a. accomplishment.
   - ☐ b. humor.
   - ☐ c. humility.
   - ☐ d. despair.

9. The last time Reggie came to the plate, he felt
   - ☐ a. insecure.
   - ☐ b. nervous.
   - ☐ c. confident.
   - ☐ d. embarrassed.

10. The author of this selection is
    - ☐ a. George Steinbrenner.
    - ☐ b. someone writing about Reggie Jackson.
    - ☐ c. Reggie Jackson.
    - ☐ d. Ron Guidry.

Comprehension Skills

1. recalling specific facts	6. making a judgment
2. retaining concepts	7. making an inference
3. organizing facts	8. recognizing tone
4. understanding the main idea	9. understanding characters
5. drawing a conclusion	10. appreciation of literary forms

Study Skills, Part One—Following is a passage with blanks where words have been omitted. Next to the passage are groups of five words, one group for each blank. Complete the passage by circling the correct word for each of the blanks.

Mastering the Text, III

Another feature of the text you will want to explore is the index. Use it to obtain hard facts about the author and his presentation.

The Index. Every textbook contains a subject index. There may be other indexes too. An author's index, for example, may allow you to look up by ___(1)___ those authorities mentioned throughout the book. The index will also list their writings and works.

(1)   number   title
           name   page   chapter

But the subject index is likely to be the only one included in your texts. It lists alphabetically aspects and ___(2)___ that were discussed in the text. The page number is given with each listing.

Based on classroom lectures or on some previous knowledge of yours in the field, ___(3)___ the author's treatment of one topic. Look through the index until you find a familiar entry. Go to the page listed and read the material. What kind of job has the author done? Did he discuss what you expected? Was his treatment too superficial? Make a couple more ___(4)___ if needed to see if the treatment is the same throughout the book. You may find that the text covers the field with more depth than you need; or, the ___(5)___ may be the case—the text is too sketchy for you. You may need to find a book that gives a more comprehensive treatment.

Of course, you may be ___(6)___ to change texts and authors. The text you have may be the assigned book for the course. But you can use other texts. If needed, find one to supplement the one you deem to be lacking, one that you can read first to make the assigned text ___(7)___ to understand. Or you may wish to read a more extensive text, along with the assigned one, to broaden your knowledge. In other words, feed your interest in the subject—find a text that works for you and keeps your interest level high.

| (2) | topics | countries |
| | names | places | circumstances |

| (3) | pursue | evaluate |
| | ignore | enjoy | follow |

| (4) | trips | challenges |
| | checks | friends | books |

| (5) | same | opposite |
| | ordinary | report | estimate |

| (6) | opposed | happy |
| | powerless | anxious | able |

| (7) | essential | harder |
| | faster | easier | optional |

Study Skills, Part Two—Read the study skills passage again, paying special attention to the lesson being taught. Then, without looking back at the passage, complete each sentence below by writing in the missing word or words. Check the Answer Key on page 108 for the answers to Study Skills, Part One, and Study Skills, Part Two.

1. Every textbook contains a _____ index.

2. The index lists topics in _____ order.

3. Each listing is given with a page _____.

4. Check to see how the author treats a subject with which you are

   _____.

5. If the text does not suit your needs, you may wish to _____ it

   with another.

16 Bloods

by Wallace Terry

Vocabulary—The five words below are from the story you are about to read. Study the words and their meanings. Then complete the ten sentences that follow, using one of the five words to fill in the blank in each sentence. Mark your answer by writing the letter of the word on the line before the sentence. Check your answers in the Answer Key on page 108.

A. fatigues: uniform worn by soldiers

B. valor: bravery

C. sporadic: occurring on an irregular basis

D. gross: outrageous, brutish, and insensitive

E. translate: to change something from one form to another; to transfer or transform

_____ 1. Because I could not _____ my thoughts about the war into words, the bitterness inside my soul began to grow.

_____ 2. The oppressive heat of Vietnam made his _____ dark with perspiration.

_____ 3. No matter how many medals one received for outstanding _____ , the fact remained that a black vet was still ill-treated.

_____ 4. No one back home wanted to hear about the _____ realities of war.

_____ 5. The soldier's mind was initially filled with ideas of patriotism and _____ .

_____ 6. As his relationships became more _____ , the soldier's loneliness and isolation from the world increased.

_____ 7. Many wartime acts are _____ but necessary for survival.

_____ 8. Some soldiers in Vietnam were subject to _____ feelings of fear.

_____ 9. Some vets did well when they reached home and were able to _____ their bitterness into positive actions.

_____ 10. The soldier was buried in his army _____ .

I left Vietnam the end of '69. I flew from An Khe to Cam Ranh Bay, still in my jungle fatigues. I hadn't bathed in six months. I had a full-grown beard. My hair was so matted against my head I couldn't pull my fingers through it. I smelled like a cockroach on Christmas. Like Mount Rushmore in the springtime. I was funky. I was really funky.

Then they put me in this big fabulous airplane. I'm sittin' there with filth all over me. From my head to my toe. I felt like I was in the Twilight Zone.

We landed in California when it was dark. We were taken to some barracks. We took a shower, and they gave us some new clothes and a steak dinner. Then I got on another plane.

The same day I left Vietnam, I was standin' back on the corner in Baltimore. Back in the States. A animal. And nobody could deal with me.

I went home. I banged on the door. About four o'clock in the morning. I'm hollerin', screamin' in the middle of the street.

"Wake up, you motherfuckers. Get out of there. I'm home. Shit."

There wasn't nobody there.

I went and found my grandparents, and they told me my parents had moved a month before and where to find them.

When I got there, my mother wouldn't even open the door. She didn't even recognize me.

I started rappin' to her, tellin' her I was her son. And she finally let me in.

It took her a long time to adjust to who I had changed to be. She had heard so much negative rumors about Vietnam vets bein' crazy. She was afraid of me.

Before I got out of the service, the My Lai stuff [news of the destruction of the village of My Lai] came out in the papers. Some of who had been in similar incidents in combat units felt that we were next. We were afraid that we were gonna be the next ones that was gonna be court-martialed or called upon to testify against someone or against themselves. A lot of us wiped out whole villages. We didn't put 'em in a ditch per se, but when you dead, you dead. If you kill 30 people and somebody else kills 29, and they happen to be in a ditch and the other 30 happen to be on top, whose guilty of the biggest atrocity? So all of us were scared. I was scared for a long time.

I got out January '71. Honorable discharge. Five Bronze Stars for valor.

I couldn't deal with goin' to school, because I wasn't motivated. The only friends I made were militant types, because they were the only ones could relate to what I was tryin' to say. I took all the money I saved up and bought weapons. Fifteen-hundred dollars' worth. Rifles, guns. I joined the Black Panthers group basically because it was a warlike group. With the Panthers we started givin' out

To the soldiers who fought it, Vietnam was an insane test, a nightmare war. Yet, some men came home to an even tougher battle.

free milk and other community help things. But I was thinkin' we needed a revolution. A physical revolution. And I was thinkin' about Vietnam. All the time.

I could never have a permanent-type relationship with a lady. It was always sporadic-type relationships. They couldn't understand what I was goin' through when the flashbacks started. Tryin' to talk to them, they wouldn't wanna hear it. Didn't want to hear no gross war stories. Hear about dead people. I just couldn't translate my feelings to a lady.

I couldn't discuss the war with my father even though he had two tours in Vietnam and was stationed in the Mekong Delta when I was there. He was a staff sergeant. A lifer. Truck driver. Jeep driver or somethin'. In a support unit with the 9th Division. I couldn't come to terms with him being in a noncombat unit. He died three years ago. He was forty-five. He had a disease he caught from the service called alcoholism. He died of alcoholism. And we never talked about Vietnam.

But my moms, she brought me back 'cause she loved me. And I think because I loved her. She kept reminding me what type of person I was before I left. Of the dreams I had promised her before I left. To help her buy a home and make sure that we was secure in life.

And she made me see the faces again. See Vietnam. See the incidents. She made me really get ashamed of myself for doin' the things I had done. You think no crime is a crime durin' war, 'specially when you get away with it. And when she made me look back at it, it just didn't seem it was possible for me to be able to do those things to other people, because I value life. That's what moms and grandmoms taught me as a child.

I've had a lotta different, short-lived jobs since I been back. I've been into drug counseling in Baltimore City Hospital. Worked in the children's clinic at Johns Hopkins Hospital. In welfare rights as a community organizer. Always human service work.

I don't have a job now. But I would take any human service job, especially where I could show the black kids and the black people that we ought to stop looking toward the stars and start looking toward each other. That our greatest horizons is in our children. And if we don't bring our children up to believe in themselves, then we'll never have anything to believe in.

But they turn their backs on a lot of us Vietnam vet'rans. They say the only way to success is through education. I wanna go back to school and get my B.A., but I can't afford to. I gotta get out there and get a job. Ain't no jobs out there. So what I'm gon' do now? Only thing else I know how to do is pick up a gun. Then I'm stupid. I'm being stupid again. I'm not going forward. I'm going backwards. And can't go any further backwards. I done been so damn far back, I'm listenin' to the echoes in the tunnel.

One day I'm down on Oliver and Milton Avenue. Go

in this grocery store. In my neighborhood.

This Vietn'ese owns the store.

He say, "I know you?"

I say, "You know me from where?"

"You Vietnam?"

"Yeah, I was in Vietnam."

"When you Vietnam."

" '68, '69."

"Yeah, me know you. An Khe. You be [in the village of] An Khe?"

"Yeah, I was in An Khe."

"Yeah, me know you. You Montagnard Man."

Ain't that some shit?

I'm buyin' groceries from him.

I ain't been in the store since. I'm still pissed off.

He's got a business, good home, drivin' cars. An I'm still strugglin'.

I'm not angry 'cause he Vietn'ese. I don't have anything against the Vietn'ese. Nothin'. Not a damn thing. I'm angry with America. When the Vietn'ese first came here, they were talkin' 'bout the new niggers. But they don't treat them like niggers. They treat them like people. If they had gave me some money to start my life over again, I'd been in a hell of a better situation than I am right now. We went to war to serve the country in what we thought was its best interest. Then America puts them above us. It's a crime. It's a crime against us.

Me and some vet'rans started what we call Base Camp One. We met at this church. It's to bring the comradeship that we had in the service into civilian life. To get a positive foundation to grow on. Because we feel that we are still in a combat situation.

We talk about the old enemy. The war. Our lives. The ghosts. The nightmares.

We didn't gain no respect for the Viet Cong until after we got into combat and found out that we had millions of dollars worth of equipment which s'posed to be advanced and so technical, and they were fighting us with whatever was available or whatever they could steal. I

Wallace Terry was born in New York City, educated at Brown, Chicago, and Harvard universities, and ordained in the Disciples of Christ ministry. He has produced documentary films on black Marines and served as a race relations consultant to General David C. Jones when Jones was commanding general of the United States Air Force in Europe. Terry has also been a radio and television commentator for various programs and has written for *USA TODAY.* In 1983 he was named to the Veterans Administration Advisory Committee on Readjustment Problems of Vietnam Veterans.

don't think we were well trained enough for that type of guerrilla warfare. But we were better soldiers, better equipped. And we had the technology.

In fact, we had the war beat until they started this pacification program. Don't shoot, unless shot upon. The government kept handicapping us one way or 'nother. I don't think America lost. I think they gave up. They surrendered.

And this country befell upon us one big atrocity. It lied. They had us naïve, young dumb-ass niggers believin' that this war was for democracy and independence. It was fought for money. All those big corporations made billions on the war, and then America left.

I can't speak for other minorities, but living in America in the eighties is a war for survival among black folks. And black vet'rans are being overlooked more than everybody. We can't find jobs, because nobody trusts us. Because we killers. We crazy. We went away intelligent young men to do the job of American citizens. And once we did, we came back victims.

Starting Time		Finishing Time	
Reading Time		Reading Rate	
Comprehension		Vocabulary	

Comprehension — Read the following questions and statements. For each one, put an *x* in the box before the option that contains the most complete or accurate answer. Check your answers in the Answer Key on page 108.

1. The writer's father was a
   ☐ a. staff sergeant.
   ☐ b. major.
   ☐ c. private.
   ☐ d. first lieutenant.

2. We can see from this selection that when the Vietnam veterans returned home
   ☐ a. most Americans treated them with respect.
   ☐ b. they were considered war criminals.
   ☐ c. the government honored them.
   ☐ d. many people were afraid of them.

3. The events in the story are told in
   - ☐ a. spatial order.
   - ☐ b. a comparison.
   - ☐ c. chronological order.
   - ☐ d. a simple list.

4. The main idea of the selection is that
   - ☐ a. black soldiers were victimized by the government and the people of the United States.
   - ☐ b. the Vietnam War could have been won.
   - ☐ c. all United States troops committed war crimes.
   - ☐ d. soldiers must put their bad experiences behind them.

5. From the first paragraph, it can be concluded that the climate in Vietnam is
   - ☐ a. dry and hot.
   - ☐ b. moderate and dry.
   - ☐ c. hot and humid.
   - ☐ d. cold and snowy.

6. It seems that the writer of this selection is intent upon
   - ☐ a. casting blame on other people.
   - ☐ b. understanding himself and what has happened to him.
   - ☐ c. getting even with all Vietnamese people.
   - ☐ d. leading an armed revolt.

7. We can infer that the writer of the selection
   - ☐ a. was not a good soldier.
   - ☐ b. matured early.
   - ☐ c. was an ex-convict.
   - ☐ d. was not close to his father.

8. The passage ends on a note of
   - ☐ a. bitterness.　　☐ c. contentment.
   - ☐ b. concern.　　☐ d. curiosity.

9. The writer can best be described as
   - ☐ a. lovable and loving.
   - ☐ b. sincere but troubled.
   - ☐ c. nervous but determined.
   - ☐ d. thoughtful and kind.

10. The opening sentence is
   - ☐ a. an opinion.　　☐ c. a statement of fact.
   - ☐ b. an overstatement.　　☐ d. an understatement.

Comprehension Skills

1. recalling specific facts	6. making a judgment
2. retaining concepts	7. making an inference
3. organizing facts	8. recognizing tone
4. understanding the main idea	9. understanding characters
5. drawing a conclusion	10. appreciation of literary forms

Study Skills, Part One—Following is a passage with blanks where words have been omitted. Next to the passage are groups of five words, one group for each blank. Complete the passage by circling the correct word for each of the blanks.

Mastering the Text, IV

You know from earlier discussions that previewing is the ___(1)___ reader's first step. Fortunately the organization of today's texts makes previewing quick and rewarding. Listed below are the steps to follow when previewing a textbook chapter.

PREREAD THE CHAPTER

1. Read the Title. As pointed out earlier, the title is the author's announcement of what is to come. It may in fact define the ___(2)___ of the entire chapter.

2. Read the Subheads. The subheads may list the author's three or four main points. They also may give a ___(3)___ to the significance of the forthcoming material. In either case, reading the subheads will give you a jump on the chapter.

3. Read the Illustrations. Don't just look at the illustrations, *read* them. The role of graphs, maps and charts is to present in a ___(4)___ fashion data that might otherwise take hundreds of words to cover. Graphic aids often demonstrate a relationship between two facts. That

(1)	slow	wise
	advanced　adult	foolish

(2)	limits	forecast
	outline　skill	ending

(3)	choice	clue
	motive　statement	conclusion

(4)	visual	vocal
	violent　written	audible

relationship may be the very heart of the chapter—the base upon which the entire discussion is founded. Skipping over such obviously important aids in the name of saving time can decrease understanding. That in turn *increases* the time it takes to comprehend the material completely.

4. Read the Opening Paragraph. This helps you organize the material to come. Try to see what will be ___(5)___ of you when you read.

5. Read the Closing Paragraph. Capitalize on the author's ___(6)___ words, the statements that cap the chapter.

6. Skim through the Chapter. Get the feel of the presentation. Use typographical aids such as roman numerals, headlines, italics, and capital letters. Try to pick out the three or four ___(7)___ points to be covered. In that way, the sense of the lesson will be apparent to you even before you study it.

(5)   observed   received
     expected   thought   acquired

(6)   opening   favorite
     initial   hidden   parting

(7)   repeated   main
     simple   difficult   marginal

Study Skills, Part Two—Read the study skills passage again, paying special attention to the lesson being taught. Then, without looking back at the passage, complete each sentence below by writing in the missing word or words. Check the Answer Key on page 108 for the answers to Study Skills, Part One, and Study Skills, Part Two.

1. The _____ of today's texts makes previewing fast and helpful.

2. The title and _____ will give you an idea of what the chapter covers.

3. The belief that visual aids are not important for increasing understanding is _____ .

4. Read the opening and _____ paragraphs to give you a better understanding of the chapter's scope.

5. The last step in previewing is to _____ through the chapter.

17 | Let the Trumpet Sound

by Stephen B. Oates

Vocabulary—The five words below are from the story you are about to read. Study the words and their meanings. Then complete the ten sentences that follow, using one of the five words to fill in the blank in each sentence. Mark your answer by writing the letter of the word on the line before the sentence. Check your answers in the Answer Key on page 108.

A. usurped: taken by force; seized, often wrongfully

B. tactics: strategic means for achieving a purpose

C. hoax: an imaginary story that is used for deception

D. haven: a safe place

E. brooded: dwelt upon with respect or sorrow

_____ 1. Some of the older leaders in the town saw their positions being _____ by the younger, more aggressive, newcomers.

_____ 2. In quiet agony, the leader _____ over the troubles of his race.

_____ 3. The _____ was started by a small group of radicals who did not agree with the majority.

_____ 4. For years, the old man _____ over the loss of his only son.

_____ 5. When the leader's position was _____ , chaos ensued.

_____ 6. The church became a _____ for the runaway slave.

_____ 7. The devious _____ used to seize power were devised by a mastermind.

_____ 8. Only logical _____ were used to win the war.

_____ 9. The inner city is a _____ for no one, black or white.

_____ 10. Many were hurt by the ill-conceived _____ of the underground rebels.

After Christmas, whites resorted to psychological warfare to break the boycott, hinting at violence, trying to sow dissension among leaders and followers alike. Whites circulated rumors that King himself was pocketing MIA money, that he had bought himself a big new Cadillac and his wife a Buick station wagon. Prominent whites also told older, more established Negro preachers that their positions had been usurped by "these young upstarts" and that they should be the protest leaders. By now, the boycott was commanding national attention and thrusting King into the headlines. And this reactivated the "self-defeating rivalries" that had afflicted the black community before the protest. Jealous of King and hostile to seminary-trained ministers in general, a lot of "anti-intellectual" preachers, who were called to the pulpit by divine inspiration, griped and groaned that King was using the movement to get attention and enrich himself.

"I almost broke down under the continual battering of this argument," King recalled. When other MIA leaders began repeating it themselves, King called an emergency meeting and offered his resignation. "I am willing to decrease so that others may increase," he told them. "Maybe a more mature person can bring about a speedier conclusion." His colleagues were shocked. Aware that the people probably would not follow anyone but King, they assured him that they were pleased with his leadership and unanimously urged him to remain. After the meeting, King drove to the parsonage "more at peace than I had been in some time."

As January passed, the city fathers turned to more devious tactics. They lured three unsuspecting Negro preachers to a city commission meeting, then on January 22 announced to the press that a settlement had been reached with Negro leaders and that the boycott was over. When King heard about the hoax, he was incredulous. Clearly he had more to learn about the sneakiness of segregationists. Quickly he sent word out to black Montgomery that the announcement was a lie. The next morning, Negro paperboys aroused their clients and warned them not to believe "that stuff about the boycott on the front page." King and others confronted the three ministers, who repudiated the newspaper story, and King himself publicly announced that the boycott was still on.

After that the mayor went on television and warned that the city commission was going to "stop pussy-footing around with the boycott." Then the police started harassing the car pool, threatening to arrest Negro drivers, revoke their licenses, and cancel their insurance policies. One dreary January evening, King was on his way home when two motorcycle cops arrested him for speeding. A patrol car came and took him away. Alone in the back seat, King panicked. The car was heading in the opposite direction from downtown, where he thought the jail was located.

Daily, Martin Luther King faced hatred and death. Alone, weary . . . how could he keep a moment of weakness from slipping into surrender?

Presently the driver turned onto a dark and dingy street and headed under a bridge. King was certain that the cops were going "to dump me off" in some remote place. "But this can't be," he thought. "These men are officers of the law." But the law was white man's law, and he feared that a mob was waiting on the other side of the bridge. He was going to be murdered and mutilated. The cops would claim that the mob had overpowered them. . . .

As the car moved past the bridge, King braced himself, certain that he was approaching his doom. But when he looked up, he saw a light in the distance and gradually made out the sign: "Montgomery Jail." He let out a sigh of relief, for "going to jail at that moment seemed like going to some safe haven."

Inside, the jailer booked and threw him into a large cell with many others. As he stood there, "strange gusts of emotion swept through me like cold winds," King said. For the first time in his life, he was behind bars, and he felt profoundly disoriented, for his father had taught him to have an Old Testament respect for the law. But remember what Thoreau said. "Under a government which imprisons any unjustly, the true place for a just man is also a prison." "The real road to happiness," Gandhi said, "lies in going to jail and undergoing suffering and privations there in the interest of one's country and religion."

King found himself with drunks, vagrants, and thieves, all thrown together in democratic misery. They lay on cots with torn-up mattresses, relieved themselves in a naked toilet in the corner. The place reeked of urine and sweat. No matter what these men have done, King thought, "they shouldn't be treated like this."

The jailer came and led him down a long corridor into a small room at the front. Here the police fingerprinted him "like a criminal." Meanwhile Ralph Abernathy had tried to sign King's bond and a crowd of Negroes had gathered in front of the jail. Intimidated, the police released King on his own recognizance and told him his trial would be held on Monday morning. All this for a minor traffic violation! King would be found guilty, of course. But at home, in the company of his wife, church members, and MIA friends, King felt strong again, knowing that he did not stand alone.

By late January, King was receiving thirty to forty hate letters a day. Some were signed from the "KKK," warning him to "get out of town or else." Others were crudely lettered threats on his life. "You old son of a bitch," read one missive from a Montgomery white citizen, "did you know you only have a very short time to life if you dont quit your dam foolishness here in Montgomery? You old goddam son of a bitch when you think you as good as white people you are sadly mistaken. . . . If you don't

heed this warning it will be kayo for you and your gang."
"You niggers are getting your self in a bad place," another letter said. "We need and will have a Hitler to get our country straightened out."

Then there were the obscene phone calls—as many as twenty-five a day now. Sometimes there was only the hawk of a throat, the sound of spit against the receiver. Other callers would curse and rave, accusing King of lusting after white women, of wanting to perform "incredible degeneracies." Still others threatened not only to murder King, but to wipe out his wife and daughter too. King could not bear such phone calls. He had no right to put his family in such danger. He saw how upset Coretta was, for she had to answer the phone when he was gone, and the threats were getting to her, too. But they did not dare take the phone off the hook lest they miss some urgent call about the boycott. It was getting so bad they both jumped when the phone went off.

One day a friend reported from reliable sources that a plan was afoot to have King assassinated. King admitted that he was "scared to death," worn down by "the freezing and paralyzing effect" of fear. He found himself at a mass meeting, trying to give an impression of strength. "If one day you find me sprawled out dead, I do not want you to retaliate with a single act of violence. I urge you to continue protesting with the same dignity and discipline you have shown so far." A strange hush fell over the church. Afterward, Abernathy said, "Something is wrong. You are disturbed about something." But King was evasive. "Martin, you were not talking about some general principle," Abernathy said. "You had something specific in mind." For the first time, King confided in Abernathy about the threats on his life and family. Abernathy tried to help, to say something comforting, but King was still afraid.

He found himself wishing that there might be "an honorable way out without injuring the cause." He would look at Coretta and Yoki and freeze with fear: *they can be taken away from me at any moment.*

One night he came home late from an MIA meeting. Exhausted, he crawled into bed and tried to sleep, knowing that he had to get up early "to keep things going." The phone rang. Steeling himself, he picked up the receiver. On the other end was a furious voice, "an ugly voice," and it cut through King like a dagger, "Nigger, if you aren't out of this town in three days we gonna blow your brains out and blow up your house." There was a click.

King rose and walked the floor. He thought about all the things he had studied in college, the philosophical and theological discourses on sin and evil, and realized that he couldn't take it any more: the calls, the threats, this awful fear. He went into the kitchen and put on a pot of coffee. Yes, he had to quit. There was no other choice. He watched the coffee perk, poured a cup, and

A professional biographer, Stephen B. Oates has researched and written biographies of Nat Turner, John Brown, Abraham Lincoln, William Faulkner, and Martin Luther King, Jr. In writing *Let the Trumpet Sound,* Oates utilized the Martin Luther King Collection at Boston University, collections at the Martin Luther King, Jr. Center for Nonviolent Social Change, in Atlanta, and other public and private sources.

sat down at the table. He brooded on how he could step down without appearing to be a coward. He thought about Coretta and Yoki—"the darling of my life"—and felt weak and terribly alone. Then he heard something say to him, "You can't call on Daddy now. He's up in Atlanta a hundred and seventy-five miles away. You can't even call on Momma now."

He put his head in his hands and bowed over the table. "Oh Lord," he prayed aloud, "I'm down here trying to do what is right. But, Lord, I must confess that I'm weak now. I'm afraid. The people are looking to me for leadership, and if I stand before them without strength and courage, they too will falter. I am at the end of my powers. I have nothing left. I can't face it alone."

He sat there, his head still bowed in his hands, tears burning his eyes. But then he felt something—a presence, a stirring in himself. And it seemed that an inner voice was speaking to him with quiet assurance: "Martin Luther, stand up for righteousness. Stand up for justice. Stand up for truth. And, lo, I will be with you, even unto the end of the world." He saw lightning flash. He heard thunder roar. It was the voice of Jesus telling him *still* to fight on. And "he promised never to leave me, never to leave me alone. No, never alone, No, never alone. He promised never to leave me, never to leave me alone. . . ."

He raised his head. He felt stronger now. He could face the morrow. Whatever happened, God in His wisdom meant it to be. King's trembling stopped, and he felt an inner calm he had never experienced before. He realized that "I can stand up without fear. I can face anything." And for the first time God was profoundly real and personal to him. The idea of a personal God was no longer some "metaphysical category" he found philosophically and theologically satisfying. No, God was very close to him now, a living God who could transform "the fatigue of despair into the buoyancy of hope" and who would never, ever, leave him alone.

Starting Time		*Finishing Time*	
Reading Time		*Reading Rate*	
Comprehension		*Vocabulary*	

Comprehension— Read the following questions and statements. For each one, put an *x* in the box before the option that contains the most complete or accurate answer. Check your answers in the Answer Key on page 108.

1. The boycott described in this selection took place in
   - ☐ a. Atlanta.
   - ☐ b. Newark.
   - ☐ c. Montgomery.
   - ☐ d. Detroit.

2. From this selection we learn that
   - ☐ a. King was a fearless man.
   - ☐ b. policemen are always just.
   - ☐ c. Ralph Abernathy disliked King.
   - ☐ d. the KKK opposed King.

3. The events in the selection are related in
   - ☐ a. a cause-and-effect situation.
   - ☐ b. chronological order.
   - ☐ c. a simple listing.
   - ☐ d. a compare-and-contrast manner.

4. Which of the following best states the main thought of this selection?
   - ☐ a. No rest for the weary
   - ☐ b. Never say die
   - ☐ c. Here today, gone tomorrow
   - ☐ d. Keeping time to the beat

5. In order to break the boycott, the whites tried to
   - ☐ a. assassinate King.
   - ☐ b. legally stop King.
   - ☐ c. discredit King.
   - ☐ d. kidnap King.

6. We can make the judgment that
   - ☐ a. in some cases, the law is unjust.
   - ☐ b. blacks actually enjoyed segregation.
   - ☐ c. many whites aided King's boycott.
   - ☐ d. King was involved in city politics.

7. This selection implies that Ralph Abernathy was King's
   - ☐ a. professor.
   - ☐ b. minister.
   - ☐ c. friend.
   - ☐ d. uncle.

8. The tone of the last paragraph helps reveal that King was
   - ☐ a. uncertain.
   - ☐ b. determined.
   - ☐ c. unrealistic.
   - ☐ d. sarcastic.

9. What do the last three paragraphs reveal about King's character?
   - ☐ a. He was humorous.
   - ☐ b. He was shallow and selfish.
   - ☐ c. He was fearless.
   - ☐ d. He was thoughtful and religious.

10. This selection is probably part of
    - ☐ a. a biography.
    - ☐ b. a legal document.
    - ☐ c. an essay.
    - ☐ d. a diary.

Comprehension Skills

1. recalling specific facts	6. making a judgment
2. retaining concepts	7. making an inference
3. organizing facts	8. recognizing tone
4. understanding the main idea	9. understanding characters
5. drawing a conclusion	10. appreciation of literary forms

Study Skills, Part One—Following is a passage with blanks where words have been omitted. Next to the passage are groups of five words, one group for each blank. Complete the passage by circling the correct word for each of the blanks.

Marking the Text

If you ___(1)___ your textbook you will want to write in it. Marking the text as you read is creative reading— it is motivating and stimulating. It can be the most creative reading you do.

Don't make the mistake of some students—that of frequent highlighting. Many students feel that they should highlight important facts and information. But as they read, almost everything they encounter seems to be important and ___(2)___ of being highlighted. If you look

(1)
        rent   own
lease   borrow   steal

(2)
        worthy   wary
hopeful   desirous   afraid

at a book owned by a student who has this habit, you will find that almost a third of every chapter is marked. In such a case, the highlighting is so distracting that the eye actually seeks out the ___(3)___ passages to read.

In other words, you must mark selectively. Highlight only those passages that are of extreme importance, and use some more methods of marking the text that are effective and not distracting. For instance, if you wish to set off an important line or passage, use the abbreviation *imp.* in the margin. You can also use circles, numbers and brackets to effectively ___(4)___ your text.

Brackets are used in much the same way as highlighting to mark off very ___(5)___ statements. Look for such statements at the start of each new division. A strong summary statement is a good candidate for bracketing too. But remember, use brackets sparingly.

Circles and numbers are used to indicate important series and enumerations. Circle the key word that begins the series, then number the items in the series. You do that to help you find the list later. Many times explanations and details accompany a list, and the items may be sentences, paragraphs or even ___(6)___ apart.

Abbreviations are used to indicate the principal statement *(imp.)* of the whole lesson; a major illustration *(ill.)* that helps the reader ___(7)___ an essential concept; and a conclusion *(con.)* based on facts and data included in the chapter.

| (3) | bright | | dull |
| | unmarked | marked | scribbled |

| (4) | mark | | recall |
| | destroy | improve | write |

| (5) | frequent | | important |
| | scarce | biased | true |

| (6) | pages | | chapters |
| | books | inches | rooms |

| (7) | regret | | predict |
| | understand | enjoy | control |

Study Skills, Part Two—Read the study skills passage again, paying special attention to the lesson being taught. Then, without looking back at the passage, complete each sentence below by writing in the missing word or words. Check the Answer Key on page 108 for the answers to Study Skills, Part One, and Study Skills, Part Two.

1. Marking the text as you read can be the most _____ reading you do.

2. Don't make the mistake of highlighting too _____ .

3. _____ may be used to mark off statements at the beginning and end of each division.

4. Circle the key words, and _____ the items in a series.

5. Imp., ill., and con. are _____ you may use.

by Richard Wright

Vocabulary—The five words below are from the story you are about to read. Study the words and their meanings. Then complete the ten sentences that follow, using one of the five words to fill in the blank in each sentence. Mark your answer by writing the letter of the word on the line before the sentence. Check your answers in the Answer Key on page 108.

A. indulgently: leniently, not at all strictly

B. burned: became angered, fumed

C. toyed: played with, fussed with

D. remote: faraway, distant

E. shunt: to turn aside; to forget about

_____ 1. The principal smiled _____ and said nothing about my sarcastic remark.

_____ 2. With tears in his eyes, the child tried to _____ memories of past abuses from his mind.

_____ 3. The teacher _____ with the papers on her desk as she half listened to the student's excuses.

_____ 4. There was a thoughtful, _____ look on the student's face as he emerged from the principal's office.

_____ 5. The boy _____ at the thought of the unkind remarks leveled against him.

_____ 6. In no time at all the boy was able to _____ all past happenings from his memory and focus only on the present.

_____ 7. While being reprimanded, the youngster nervously _____ with the lock of hair that would never stay in place.

_____ 8. After separating the two fighting boys, the mother _____ took her son's hand and quietly led him to the car.

_____ 9. The unruly crowd _____ over the injustice; later they would call for the mayor's resignation.

_____ 10. Slowly, the dying man closed his eyes and spoke in a _____ whisper.

The school term ended. I was selected as valedictorian of my class and assigned to write a paper to be delivered at one of the public auditoriums. One morning the principal summoned me to his office.

"Well, Richard Wright, here's your speech," he said with smooth bluntness and shoved a stack of stapled sheets across his desk.

"What speech?" I asked as I picked up the papers.

"The speech you're to say the night of graduation," he said.

"But, professor, I've written my speech already," I said.

He laughed confidently, indulgently.

"Listen, boy, you're going to speak to both *white* and colored people that night. What can you alone think of saying to them? You have no experience . . ."

I burned.

"I know that I'm not educated, professor," I said, "But the people are coming to hear the students, and I won't make a speech that you've written."

He leaned back in his chair and looked at me in surprise.

"You know, we've never had a boy in this school like you before," he said. "You've had your way around here. Just how you managed to do it, I don't know. But, listen, take this speech and say it. I know what's best for you. You can't afford to just say *anything* before those white people that night." He paused and added meaningfully: "The superintendent of schools will be there; you're in a position to make a good impression on him. I've been a principal for more years than you are old, boy. I've seen many a boy and girl graduate from this school, and none of them was too proud to recite a speech I wrote for them."

I had to make up my mind quickly; I was faced with a matter of principle. I wanted to graduate, but I did not want to make a public speech that was not my own.

"Professor, I'm going to say my own speech that night," I said.

He grew angry.

"You're just a young, hotheaded fool," he said. He toyed with a pencil and looked up at me. "Suppose you don't graduate?"

"But I passed my examinations," I said.

"Look, mister," he shot at me, "I'm the man who says who passes at this school."

I was so astonished that my body jerked. I had gone to this school for two years and I had never suspected what kind of man the principal was; it simply had never occurred to me to wonder about him.

"Then I don't graduate," I said flatly.

I turned to leave.

"Say, you. Come here," he called.

I turned and faced him; he was smiling at me in a remote, superior sort of way.

Which speech to deliver? The principal's was good but false; Richard's was true but could cost him his future.

"You know, I'm glad I talked to you," he said. "I was seriously thinking of placing you in the school system, teaching. But, now, I don't think that you'll fit."

He was tempting me, baiting me; this was the technique that snared black young minds into supporting the southern way of life.

"Look, professor, I may never get a chance to go to school again," I said. "But I like to do things right."

"What do you mean?"

"I've no money. I'm going to work. Now, this ninth-grade diploma isn't going to help me much in life. I'm not bitter about it; it's not your fault. But I'm just not going to do things this way."

"Have you talked to anybody about this?" he asked me.

"No, why?"

"Are you sure?"

"This is the first I've heard of it, professor," I said, amazed again.

"You haven't talked to any white people about this?"

"No, sir!"

"I just wanted to know," he said.

My amazement increased; the man was afraid now for his job!

"Professor, you don't understand me." I smiled.

"You're just a young, hot fool," he said, confident again. "Wake up, boy. Learn the world you're living in. You're smart and I know what you're after. I've kept closer track of you than you think. I know your relatives. Now, if you play safe," he smiled and winked, "I'll help you to go to school, to college."

"I want to learn, professor," I told him. "But there are some things I don't want to know."

"Good-bye," he said.

I went home, hurt but determined. I had been talking to a "bought" man and he had tried to "buy" me. I felt that I had been dealing with something unclean. That night Griggs, a boy who had gone through many classes with me, came to the house.

"Look, Dick, you're throwing away your future here in Jackson," he said. "Go to the principal, talk to him, take his speech and say it. I'm saying the one he wrote. So why can't you? What the hell? What can you lose?"

"No," I said.

"Why?"

"I know only a hell of a little, but my speech is going to reflect that," I said.

"Then you're going to be blacklisted for teaching jobs," he said.

"Who the hell said I was going to teach?" I asked.

"God, but you've got a will," he said.

"It's not will. I just don't want to do things that way," I said.

He left. Two days later Uncle Tom came to me. I knew

that the principal had called him in.

"I hear that the principal wants you to say a speech which you've rejected," he said.

"Yes, sir. That's right," I said.

"May I read the speech you've written?" he asked.

"Certainly," I said, giving him my manuscript.

"And may I see the one that the principal wrote?"

I gave him the principal's speech too. He went to his room and read them. I sat quiet, waiting. He returned.

"The principal's speech is the better speech," he said.

"I don't doubt it," I replied. "But why did they ask me to write a speech if I can't deliver it?"

"Would you let me work on your speech?" he asked.

"No, sir."

"Now, look, Richard, this is your future . . ."

"Uncle Tom, I don't care to discuss this with you," I said.

He stared at me, then left. The principal's speech was simpler and clearer than mine, but it did not say anything; mine was cloudy, but it said what I wanted to say. What could I do? I had half a mind not to show up at the graduation exercises. I was hating my environment more each day. As soon as school was over, I would get a job, save money, and leave.

Griggs, who had accepted a speech written by the principal, came to my house each day and we went off into the woods to practice orating; day in and day out we spoke to the trees, to the creeks, frightening the birds, making the cows in the pastures stare at us in fear. I memorized my speech so thoroughly that I could have recited it in my sleep.

The news of my clash with the principal had spread through the class and the students became openly critical of me.

"Richard, you're a fool. You're throwing away every chance you've got. If they had known the kind of fool boy you are, they would never have made you valedictorian," they said.

I gritted my teeth and kept my mouth shut, but my rage was mounting by the hour. My classmates, motivated by a desire to "save" me, pestered me until I all but reached the breaking point. In the end the principal had to caution them to let me alone, for fear I would throw up the sponge and walk out.

I had one more problem to settle before I could make my speech. I was the only boy in my class wearing short pants and I was grimly determined to leave school in long pants. Was I not going to work? Would I not be on my own? When my desire for long pants became known at home, yet another storm shook the house.

"You're trying to go too fast," my mother said.

"You're nothing but a child," Uncle Tom pronounced.

"He's beside himself," Granny said.

I served notice that I was making my own decisions from then on. I borrowed money from Mrs. Bibbs, my employer, made a down payment on a pearl-gray suit. If I could not pay for it, I would take the damn thing back after graduation.

On the night of graduation I was nervous and tense; I rose and faced the audience and my speech rolled out. When my voice stopped there was some applause. I did not care if they liked it or not; I was through. Immediately, even before I left the platform, I tried to shunt all memory of the event from me. A few of my classmates managed to shake my hand as I pushed toward the door, seeking the street. Somebody invited me to a party and I did not accept. I did not want to see any of them again. I walked home, saying to myself: The hell with it! With almost seventeen years of baffled living behind me, I faced the world in 1925.

Richard Wright was born near Natchez, Mississippi, in 1908. He moved to Chicago in 1927 and to New York City in 1937. He lived in Paris from 1946 until his death in 1960.

Wright became famous in the 1950s upon the publication of his first novel, *Native Son*, which initiated the genre of the black protest novel. *Native Son* was the first bestseller written by a black person and the first Book-of-the-Month Club selection by a black author.

Wright's other novels include *The Outsider* and *The Long Dream*. His autobiography, *Black Boy*, realistically depicts black life in the United States in the early twentieth century.

Starting Time ☐   *Finishing Time* ☐

Reading Time ☐   *Reading Rate* ☐

Comprehension ☐   *Vocabulary* ☐

Comprehension— Read the following questions and statements. For each one, put an *x* in the box before the option that contains the most complete or accurate answer. Check your answers in the Answer Key on page 108.

1. Griggs was Richard's
   ☐ a. brother.
   ☐ b. classmate.
   ☐ c. cousin.
   ☐ d. employer.

2. This whole selection points to the fact that Richard
   ☐ a. had a mind of his own.
   ☐ b. was a violent person.
   ☐ c. lacked self-confidence.
   ☐ d. disliked school.

3. Richard's initial refusal to give any speech but his own resulted in threats about future jobs from the principal. That is an example of
   ☐ a. cause and effect.
   ☐ b. order of importance.
   ☐ c. time order.
   ☐ d. comparison and contrast.

4. Which of the following best applies to the way everyone but Richard felt?
   ☐ a. Variety is the spice of life.
   ☐ b. Look before you leap.
   ☐ c. Beauty is as beauty does.
   ☐ d. Don't rock the boat.

5. When the principal did not get his own way he
   ☐ a. relished the prospect of what would happen to Richard.
   ☐ b. easily gave in to Richard.
   ☐ c. simply ignored Richard.
   ☐ d. began to feel a bit threatened himself.

6. The writer of this article was probably born in
   ☐ a. 1900.   ☐ c. 1916.
   ☐ b. 1909.   ☐ d. 1925.

7. We can surmise that Richard
   ☐ a. liked playing games.
   ☐ b. enjoyed causing trouble.
   ☐ c. was a smart student.
   ☐ d. respected the principal.

8. The narrator's tone is one of
   ☐ a. sorrow.   ☐ c. defiance.
   ☐ b. security.   ☐ d. curiosity.

9. We can easily see that Richard was
   ☐ a. a young man with principles.
   ☐ b. a follower.
   ☐ c. highly organized.
   ☐ d. openly creative.

10. This selection is probably part of
    ☐ a. a play.   ☐ c. a biography.
    ☐ b. a poem.   ☐ d. an autobiography.

Comprehension Skills

1. recalling specific facts	6. making a judgment
2. retaining concepts	7. making an inference
3. organizing facts	8. recognizing tone
4. understanding the main idea	9. understanding characters
5. drawing a conclusion	10. appreciation of literary forms

Study Skills, Part One—Following is a passage with blanks where words have been omitted. Next to the passage are groups of five words, one group for each blank. Complete the passage by circling the correct word for each of the blanks.

Comprehension and Reading, I

Reading is both a visual and a mental skill. The visual parts involve seeing the words and ___(1)___ the eyes. The mental activities call for recognizing the organization of the letters and understanding the ___(2)___ . The first skills needed for thorough comprehension are word recognition skills.

Once the word has been seen, it must be recognized if it is to be understood. We recognize words by remembering them, pronouncing them, or analyzing

(1)   checking   washing
     rolling   closing   moving

(2)   person   thought
     word   mind   reason

them. The words we recall are those in our sight vocabulary. Those are the words we see often enough to recognize on sight. You may recall __(3)__ lists of "sight words" in the early grades of school. Good readers—sight readers—have developed a large vocabulary of words that they recognize at once when reading. Such readers slow down to sound out or pronounce only when they come to a new and __(4)__ word. Frequently in reading clinics and reading improvement courses, projectors are used to flash sight words on the screen for fractions of a second. That training is designed to enhance and reinforce the reader's stock of sight words.

The second way we recognize words is by pronouncing them. We do this for words that are not part of our sight vocabulary but are in our __(5)__ vocabulary. They are words we recognize when we hear them spoken aloud. Our knowledge of phonics helps us to pronounce unfamiliar words—that is why phonics skills are valuable.

The third technique we use in word recognition is analysis, which means breaking a word down into recognizable __(6)__ . Our knowledge of syllabication and word parts helps us do this.

Reading programs that feature only one __(7)__ of attacking new words shortchange the student. To become competent readers, we need to use all the recognition skills.

(3)	dividing		memorizing
	reading	spelling	producing

(4)	dramatic		abstract
	exciting	interesting	unfamiliar

(5)	listening		reading
	spelling	working	writing

(6)	partners		parts
	looks	lessons	places

(7)	outline		picture
	question	situation	method

Study Skills, Part Two—Read the study skills passage again, paying special attention to the lesson being taught. Then, without looking back at the passage, complete each sentence below by writing in the missing word or words. Check the Answer Key on page 108 for the answers to Study Skills, Part One, and Study Skills, Part Two.

1. Reading is both a visual and a _____ skill.

2. The words we remember are those in our _____ vocabulary.

3. Good readers have a large vocabulary of words that they _____ immediately when reading.

4. Our knowledge of _____ helps us to pronounce unfamiliar words.

5. The technique called _____ means breaking a word into recognizable parts.

Lay Bare the Heart, I

by James Farmer

Vocabulary—The five words below are from the story you are about to read. Study the words and their meanings. Then complete the ten sentences that follow, using one of the five words to fill in the blank in each sentence. Mark your answer by writing the letter of the word on the line before the sentence. Check your answers in the Answer Key on page 108.

A. specter: ghost; something that haunts the mind

B. infiltrated: quietly gained access to

C. feeble: weak

D. itinerary: the proposed route or outline of a journey

E. implicitly: unquestionably, without doubt

_____ 1. The KKK meeting was well-guarded and as a result was not easily _____ .

_____ 2. The bodyguards were well-trained professionals who could be trusted _____ .

_____ 3. Bogalusa was the first stop on the speaker's _____ .

_____ 4. Death was a constant _____ , a silent companion on every trip.

_____ 5. The leader was _____ respected by every member of the group.

_____ 6. Two unmarked cars _____ the president's caravan.

_____ 7. From the _____ , we could tell exactly how long the trip would take.

_____ 8. In a _____ voice, the boy tried to explain the broken window.

_____ 9. The frightened child made a _____ attempt to display a courageous spirit.

_____ 10. The _____ of doom descended upon the crowd, smothering all hope like a thick woolen blanket.

The specter of sudden death was a constant companion in those years, riding with me on every trip. It was, therefore, no surprise when, one afternoon in 1964, a call came to my office from John Malone, the regional director of the FBI in New York.

"Mr. Farmer," he said, "I would appreciate it if you'd let me know the next time you're going to Louisiana. In fact, the next time you're going below the Mason-Dixon line."

"Why?" I asked.

"The Klan met yesterday in Bogalusa and decided that next time you come down there, you're going to be killed."

"How do you know that?" I asked.

"Routinely," he said. "We've infiltrated the Klan. We had a man there."

The threats of death came so frequently that they always had an air of unreality. I made a feeble attempt at humor: "Well, tell me, were there any dissenting votes?"

"I think you should be serious, Mr. Farmer," he replied. "The Klan is deadly serious. Until further notice, just have your secretary give me a call whenever you're going south, and let me know your itinerary."

"She won't have to call you. I can tell you now. I'm going down there tomorrow."

"To Louisiana?" he asked.

"Yes, to Bogalusa."

He sighed audibly and asked, "Okay, what airline? What flight? What time?"

After I hung up, I sat at my desk for a few minutes in contemplation. Should I cancel the trip, or at least postpone it? I had told the local black community in Bogalusa that I would be there in two days to address a freedom rally at the Baptist church. How could I cancel out of fear when they lived under the shadow of the Klan every minute of every day? I would have to go.

I called Lula and asked if she had paid last month's premium on my life insurance.

"Yes," she answered. "I mailed it yesterday."

When informed of the conversation I had had with the FBI regional director, she said, "Do you think you should go?"

Before I could reply, she answered her own question: "Yes, of course. You have to go."

I summoned key members of my staff into the office and brought them up to date. Someone mentioned something about a bulletproof vest and I rejected the idea out of hand.

"This is midsummer," I said. "Bogalusa will be like a steam bath even without that kind of paraphernalia. Furthermore, would we have similar protection for all the local people who'll be with me in that church?"

Before our meeting was over Marvin Rich said, "Although the Klan may be bluffing, I do think we should call the police in Bogalusa and alert them to the fact that

When James Farmer penetrated the heart of Klan country to address a freedom rally, he received police protection— provided by the same police who had tried to kill him a year earlier.

this threat has been made. They may want to take some precautions of their own."

The flight to New Orleans was uneventful. After taxiing to the gate, the pilot spoke over the public address system: "All passengers whose destination is New Orleans, please deplane at this time. James Farmer, please remain seated."

When the passengers had filed out, a grim-faced, overweight man came aboard the plane and walked toward me, displaying his credentials as he approached. He was a captain in the Louisiana State Police Department.

"Mr. Farmer," he began, "our governor received a call from Washington informing him that your life could be in danger while you're in our state. Governor McKeithen called my boss, Colonel Burbank, who's state director of public safety, and ordered him to protect your life. Colonel Burbank has assigned me that responsibility."

The plainclothes lieutenant motioned through the window of the plane and four other plainclothesmen boarded and came toward me. I must confess to a bit of apprehension, since it had been the state police and deputized red-necks who had tried to kill me a few years ago in Plaquemine, Louisiana, and the memory of that episode was still fresh.

The captain spoke again: "I'm assigning these four lieutenants as your personal bodyguards while you're in our state. They'll be with you at all times, except while you're sleeping, and even then they'll have all entrances to your room in view. They're well armed, they have a service revolver at their hips and small firearms strapped to their ankles—and they're excellent marksmen. They have two unmarked cars, one of which will transport you to Bogalusa.

"As you proceed to Bogalusa, there will be a helicopter overhead manned by state troopers armed with high-powered rifles in the event of an attempted ambush. The helicopter will be in radio communication with your four bodyguards. These lieutenants are entirely trustworthy. They're professionals who know their business. Please be assured that you can trust them implicitly. I'm holding them strictly responsible for your safety, as the governor is holding me responsible."

"Shall we go into the airport now?"

As the six of us walked to the airport, the lieutenant's eyes seemed to search everywhere danger might lurk. Inside the lobby, three black men who were standing near the entrance beckoned to me. They were friends from Bogalusa, members of the Deacons for Defense and Justice, a black self-defense organization that had been formed to shoot back when the Klan shot into homes of black citizens of Bogalusa. On a previous visit, they had told me of their plans to organize. They knew that CORE was a nonviolent organization and they said they accepted that while on CORE demonstrations. But when not on demonstrations, they would determine their response in consultation with their consciences and their God.

The KKK was said to have its largest per-capita membership in Bogalusa. On frequent occasions, carloads of white men would speed through the black community firing guns into homes, willy-nilly. The Deacons organized to fire back. After one night-riding venture by Klansmen, the Deacons returned the fire from inside their homes. The Klan cars sped away and the night riding came to an end.

I excused myself from my state police bodyguards, telling them that I wanted to talk to my friends.

"Jim," said one of the Deacons, "we don't trust those SOBs. We don't know which way they'll point their guns. We would feel much more comfortable if you'd ride to Bogalusa in our car."

"Let me work this out with the troopers," I said. "I'll be right back."

When I explained to the troopers that my friends from Bogalusa wanted me to ride in their car with them, the captain nodded.

"That will be all right as long as your friends' car is in the middle and one of ours is in front and one is behind. That way, the lieutenants will have you covered."

Our three-car caravan sped across the twenty-mile causeway spanning Lake Pontchartrain and down the concrete highway toward Bogalusa. The helicopter whirred overhead, searching the woods and hovering momentarily over roadside bars. Each time we approached one of these places, the lead car with the two lieutenants in its front seat accelerated. The Deacon driving the car in which I rode grunted as he floored his accelerator, trying to keep pace.

"Geez, that car can really fly."

Inside the town of Bogalusa, our caravan cruised to the address that had been given to the troopers. It was the home of the president of the Deacons for Defense and Justice. Before the troopers would allow me to enter the home, two of them went in and searched the house thoroughly, looking under beds, in closets, behind couches, behind

James Farmer helped establish the Congress of Racial Equality in 1942, and was its national director until 1966. He served as assistant secretary of the Department of Health, Education, and Welfare in 1969 and 1970 and has served as the program director of the National Association for the Advancement of Colored People. Farmer has also been professor of Social Welfare at Lincoln University. In 1976, Farmer became associate director of the Coalition of American Public Employees.

Farmer was born in Marshall, Texas, in 1920. He first attended college in his hometown, graduating from Wiley College in 1938. He then moved to Washington, D.C., where he received a degree from the Howard University School of Religion in 1941.

drapes, in bathrooms—everyplace an assailant could hide.

Then, one trooper said, "All right, Mr. Farmer, you can come in now."

Two of the troopers sat in the living room all night; the other two remained in one of the cars parked out front, but positioned so as to give its occupants a clear view of both windows to my bedroom, as well as the front door. Two of the Deacons waited in the living room all night, too, sitting in one corner with their guns at the ready while the troopers sat in the opposite corner with theirs.

I retired for the night, secure in the knowledge that unless a bomb were tossed through a window, the Klan could reach me only if they were prepared to swap their lives for mine.

By morning, the Deacons and the troopers in the living room were almost fraternizing. It had been a long night for them, and they'd finally agreed that one of each pair would sit guard while the others napped.

Starting Time		Finishing Time	
Reading Time		Reading Rate	
Comprehension		Vocabulary	

Comprehension— Read the following questions and statements. For each one, put an *x* in the box before the option that contains the most complete or accurate answer. Check your answers in the Answer Key on page 108.

1. Bogalusa is in
   □ a. Virginia.
   □ b. Louisiana.
   □ c. Mississippi.
   □ d. Florida.

2. The selection as a whole points to the fact that
   □ a. the KKK hated Mr. Farmer.
   □ b. policemen make good bodyguards.
   □ c. James Farmer was a Baptist minister.
   □ d. racism existed above the Mason-Dixon Line.

3. The events in the selection are presented
    ☐ a. as a simple list.
    ☐ b. in the order in which they happened.
    ☐ c. by comparing and contrasting.
    ☐ d. in numerical order.

4. Which sentence below best gives the main thought of the selection?
    ☐ a. Death was a constant companion in those years, riding with me on every trip.
    ☐ b. I summoned key members of my staff into my office and brought them up to date.
    ☐ c. The flight to New Orleans was uneventful.
    ☐ d. They'd finally agreed that one of each pair would sit guard while the others napped.

5. The way the Louisiana State Police protected Mr. Farmer shows that they were
    ☐ a. ill at ease.
    ☐ b. irresponsible.
    ☐ c. well-organized.
    ☐ d. uncooperative.

6. We can make the judgment that Mr. Farmer was
    ☐ a. confused.
    ☐ b. disgusted.
    ☐ c. obnoxious.
    ☐ d. courageous.

7. The action in this passage probably takes place in
    ☐ a. May or June.   ☐ c. September or October.
    ☐ b. July or August.   ☐ d. November or December.

8. Farmer's tone helps the reader get a sense of the trip's
    ☐ a. relaxed, holiday atmosphere.
    ☐ b. tension.
    ☐ c. length.
    ☐ d. place in history.

9 In this article, Mr. Farmer's character is mostly revealed through
    ☐ a. comments.   ☐ c. description.
    ☐ b. actions.   ☐ d. thoughts.

10. To get the reader's attention, the writer begins his story with a
    ☐ a. humorous comment.
    ☐ b. direct question.
    ☐ c. direct quote.
    ☐ d. serious statement.

Comprehension Skills	
1. recalling specific facts	6. making a judgment
2. retaining concepts	7. making an inference
3. organizing facts	8. recognizing tone
4. understanding the main idea	9. understanding characters
5. drawing a conclusion	10. appreciation of literary forms

Study Skills, Part One—Following is a passage with blanks where words have been omitted. Next to the passage are groups of five words, one group for each blank. Complete the passage by circling the correct word for each of the blanks.

Comprehension and Reading, II

Other aspects of reading comprehension follow word recognition. They are often grouped in the ___(1)___ of retention, organization, interpretation, and appreciation.

In retention, the reader is called upon to isolate details, to recall specifics, and to retain concepts. All of those skills are applied to ___(2)___ facts that have been read.

The reader is also expected to organize as he or she reads. Ways to organize are as follows:

1. Classifying. A good reader will arrange facts in groups while reading. In that way, facts that contribute to the comprehension of a concept are seen as a unit, ___(3)___ from those that deal with other concepts.

2. Establishing a Sequence. For true understanding of the author's ideas the reader must be aware of the order in which events take place. It is easier to understand a fact when it is seen as part of a related ___(4)___ . Think of each new fact as following the previous one and adding to the next.

(1)   places   objects
    countries   families   areas

(2)   remembering   enjoying
    rejecting   scattering   discarding

(3)   resulting   copied
    separate   starting   borrowed

(4)   series   division
    unit   standard   chapter

3. Following Directions. Too many readers fail to follow directions, despite the important role they play in comprehension. Following directions is an organizing skill that requires the reader to arrange facts and to understand the steps he or she must follow. Readers often do not heed directions because they are unable to ___(5)___ facts properly, or they are unable to establish a correct sequence.

4. Seeing Relationships. An author puts forth ideas in an organized fashion, presenting ___(6)___ the concepts needed to understand other, more complex concepts that follow. The reader must grasp that relationship for true comprehension.

5. Generalizing. This skill requires the reader to arrive at general rules or theories derived from the specific ___(7)___ that the author has presented.

(5)   understand   separate
      classify   estimate   appreciate

(6)   first   next
      finally   wisely   falsely

(7)   wishes   pictures
      patterns   facts   conclusions

Study Skills, Part Two—Read the study skills passage again, paying special attention to the lesson being taught. Then, without looking back at the passage, complete each sentence below by writing in the missing word or words. Check the Answer Key on page 108 for the answers to Study Skills, Part One, and Study Skills, Part Two.

1. The comprehension skill that enables the reader to recall specifics is called

   _____ .

2. Classifying is one way the reader can _____ facts.

3. To establish a sequence, the reader must be aware of the _____

   of events.

4. Following directions demands that the reader establish a _____

   sequence.

5. When the reader arrives at a rule or theory from specific facts, he is

   _____ .

Lay Bare the Heart, II

by James Farmer

Vocabulary—The five words below are from the story you are about to read. Study the words and their meanings. Then complete the ten sentences that follow, using one of the five words to fill in the blank in each sentence. Mark your answer by writing the letter of the word on the line before the sentence. Check your answers in the Answer Key on page 108.

A. **intercept:** to cut off, block

B. **stature:** a person's height when standing

C. **disperse:** to scatter in different directions

D. **residential:** having to do with places where people live

E. **imminent:** something that is about to happen immediately

_____ 1. The motorcade traveled through the city to the _____ outskirts.

_____ 2. Eventually, the crowd began to _____ .

_____ 3. With lightning speed, the police car started to _____ the pickup truck.

_____ 4. One bodyguard was of a smaller _____ than the other.

_____ 5. A shot rang out, and the marchers knew that they would have to _____ to save themselves.

_____ 6. A group of men from the KKK tried to _____ the march.

_____ 7. Jim saw his assailant's gun and recognized the threat of _____ danger.

_____ 8. Many of the houses in the _____ section of town were built over two hundred years ago.

_____ 9. The marchers breathed a sigh of relief when they saw the church; success was _____ .

_____ 10. The robber's imposing _____ easily frightened the timid store clerk.

As we drove to the church that afternoon, a pickup truck shot out from a side street and tried to intercept the car in which I was riding. The state police car behind me moved like a rocket out of the line and into the front of the pickup truck, crunching fenders with it and forcing it into a ditch. The driver of the pickup was pulled from the car and handcuffed, a pistol removed from his clothing, and he was taken away to jail. He was the leader of the local Klan organization.

Before the troopers would allow me to mount the platform at the church, they went up first, checking windows, doors, and other convenient hiding places. Two of the troopers sat in their car outside the church; the other two flanked the platform.

My address to the congregation went smoothly and I found myself whisked into the waiting car, which sped back to the New Orleans airport.

The plane had actually begun to taxi down the runway when the pilot spoke: "We are returning to the gate. All passengers will leave the aircraft immediately. Luggage will be taken off the plane and passengers will identify their luggage and search it in the presence of airline employees. We have received a call that there is a bomb aboard this plane."

No explosive was found, and in due time, we reboarded and flew uneventfully to New York.

A week later, as I returned to Bogalusa to lead a march, we went through the same ritual at the airport, with the captain introducing me to four lieutenants—two of whom were familiar faces, having been with me on the earlier visit. The other two, though somewhat smaller in stature, had huge, hamlike hands. The captain informed me that they were holders of black belts in karate.

"Why karate?" I asked.

"After your march was announced, the Klan said it was having a march the same day in Bogalusa, and it appears that the twain might meet."

The next morning, I received a call from Colonel Burbank, head of the state police.

"Mr. Farmer," he said, "I've come to town to take personal charge of your operation, because it appears it might be touch and go. After looking the situation over, it's my personal judgment that it will be very dangerous for you to be in the march this afternoon, probably suicidal."

"Colonel," I said, "I've told the local people that I'll be in the march, so I'll be there—on the front line."

"All right," he said. "We'll take all the precautions we can and I'll be in touch with you shortly."

A call came from one of the Deacons, informing me that one of their members had overheard two "crackers" talking downtown. One of them had said to the other, "This is 'D-Day.' That nigger Farmer dies today. We've got a trap set for him when his march gets downtown,

Nothing could keep James Farmer from returning to Bogalusa for a freedom march, not even an armed and dangerous Klan. But getting out of Bogalusa alive was another matter.

and there's no way he can escape. By sundown tonight, that nigger's gon' be dead and in hell."

The Deacon said, "We'll understand if you decide not to be in the march today."

"I'll be on the front line," I said.

"Okay, Jim," he said. "We'll get some of our guys as close to every intersection as the troopers will let us, and if any trouble starts, we'll be ready."

Before noon, Colonel Burbank came to the house where I was staying.

"I want to let you know what we're doing by way of security," he said. "I've ordered seventy additional state policemen into Bogalusa. I've also learned that some segregationists are planning to come down from Mississippi and others up from New Orleans for the Klan march today. So we set up road blocks at every road leading into town. Nobody, but nobody will get into this town today who can't prove that he lives here. We've cleared our downtown buildings and are stationing state policemen at key spots on rooftops and at windows in downtown buildings, all armed with high-powered rifles.

"During your march, there will be two helicopters flying overhead, manned by state police armed with high-powered rifles and powerful sound systems. If any unauthorized persons proceed toward your line of march, said persons will be ordered to halt, retreat, or disperse— whichever seems appropriate. If they disobey, the state police in the helicopters will be prepared to shoot.

"Flanking your line of march will be state police, no more than ten feet apart, armed with rifles, shotguns, and submachine guns. Immediately in front of your line of march will be an automobile, in the front seat of which will be two of your personal bodyguards, the lieutenants. If any shooting starts, drop to the ground and crawl to that car. The back door will be swung open when you get there. When you're inside the car, it will take off at high speed.

"Immediately behind you in your line of march will be your other two bodyguards, the karate men. . . . I can't think of anything that we've overlooked. Good day and good luck."

I would be lying if I said that I was not afraid. I was more terrified than at any time since Plaquemine, or maybe since the Freedom Ride from Montgomery to Mississippi. I thought about begging out, but that was clearly out of the question now. I had to go through with it.

Usually, we sang while marching—"We Shall Overcome" or "Ain't Nobody Gonna Turn Me 'Round." This time, however, we were all too scared to sing. It was a silent march. The wife of one of the Deacons, a tiny woman of about five feet and weighing about ninety pounds, insisted on marching with me on the front line. She held my arm as we marched.

When we reached downtown, it was all that Colonel Burbank had said it would be. I spotted troopers on rooftops, rifles in hand. Silhouetted at many windows were other troopers with rifles. We encountered several bands of young white men standing in little knots. They were a leather-jacketed ducktail-haircut bunch, and they seemed as scared as we were. Any second, I expected to hear the crack of a rifle. Then I remembered that, if I heard it, it meant they had missed: bullets travel faster than sound.

Silently, we walked through the business district into a residential area. The tension inside me seemed to relax a little. I thought it more likely that a shot would be fired from buildings in the downtown area. At one intersection in the residential community, eight or ten white men were standing, leaning against parked cars.

As I came next to them, one of the troopers suddenly yelled, "Hey, look out! Get him!"

Two of the troopers flanking the line of march leaped on one of the young men, taking from him a metal pipe with a large bolt on the end, which he had just drawn from his leather jacket. They disarmed him, and arrested him. I do not know whether he had intended to swing it at me. If he had, it would have crushed my skull.

At the next intersection, a trooper shouted just as suddenly, and equally loudly, "Hey! Get him!"

The police flanking my line pounced on a man in the act of drawing from his jacket a pearl-handled revolver. They arrested him, too.

Then some fool among the white toughs set off a firecracker. The troopers flanking our line of march whirled, crouched, and pointed their guns in the direction of the sound. Thinking it was a shot, I debated with myself whether to drop to the ground and try to reach the car in front of us. I decided against it; some of the marchers might panic and run for cover, and the Deacons somewhere nearby might open fire. Then all hell would break loose.

So, I stood still, as still as the death I thought was imminent.

After a time—seconds or minutes, I don't know which—one of the state troopers shouted over a bullhorn, "Apparently, it was a firecracker. Proceed with your march."

I did not relax until I was in my apartment in New York, having a drink with several members of my staff who were waiting to congratulate me on my survival.

Starting Time		Finishing Time	
Reading Time		Reading Rate	
Comprehension		Vocabulary	

Comprehension— Read the following questions and statements. For each one, put an *x* in the box before the option that contains the most complete or accurate answer. Check your answers in the Answer Key on page 108.

1. Which of the following songs did the marchers often sing?
   - ☐ a. "Sometimes I Feel like a Motherless Child"
   - ☐ b. "We Shall Overcome"
   - ☐ c. "Swing Low, Sweet Chariot"
   - ☐ d. "Great Day in the Mornin' "

2. The head of the state police felt that, despite their heavy protection, the march would be, for Farmer,
   - ☐ a. dangerous, maybe even suicidal.
   - ☐ b. all in a day's work.
   - ☐ c. necessarily shortened.
   - ☐ d. thoroughly enjoyable.

3. When Colonel Burbank told Farmer about security plans, his descriptions dealt mainly with
   - ☐ a. ascending order.
   - ☐ b. order of importance.
   - ☐ c. time order.
   - ☐ d. spatial order.

4. Choose the best alternate title for the selection.
   - ☐ a. Food for Thought
   - ☐ b. The Famous and Fearless
   - ☐ c. A March with Danger
   - ☐ d. A Police State

5. We can conclude that Mr. Farmer's permanent home is in the
   - ☐ a. North.
   - ☐ b. South.
   - ☐ c. West.
   - ☐ d. Midwest.

6. The troopers in this article were
   - ☐ a. unprofessional.
   - ☐ b. highly competent.
   - ☐ c. alarmist.
   - ☐ d. unpredictable.

7. Evidently, the bomb threat was a
   - ☐ a. rarity.
   - ☐ b. myth.
   - ☐ c. mirage.
   - ☐ d. hoax.

8. The tension produced by the selection's tone is released
   - ☐ a. near the middle of the selection.
   - ☐ b. only in the final paragraph.
   - ☐ c. nowhere in the story.
   - ☐ d. in the beginning.

9. At the end of this article, Mr. Farmer feels
   - ☐ a. relieved.
   - ☐ b. excited.
   - ☐ c. doubtful.
   - ☐ d. angry.

10. The setting of the episode is
    - ☐ a. near a lake.
    - ☐ b. on a train.
    - ☐ c. a town in the South.
    - ☐ d. a large southern university.

Comprehension Skills

1. recalling specific facts	6. making a judgment
2. retaining concepts	7. making an inference
3. organizing facts	8. recognizing tone
4. understanding the main idea	9. understanding characters
5. drawing a conclusion	10. appreciation of literary forms

Study Skills, Part One—Following is a passage with blanks where words have been omitted. Next to the passage are groups of five words, one group for each blank. Complete the passage by circling the correct word for each of the blanks.

Comprehension and Reading, III

As we have seen, retention and organization are two aspects of comprehension that are expected of the reader. Two other such areas are interpretation and appreciation. They are made up of the following six skills:

1. Understanding the Main Idea. As you would expect, proper interpretation of the material is based on understanding the main idea. Very often, though, the main idea is not ___(1)___ but must be gathered or interpreted by the reader.

2. Drawing Conclusions. Based on the ideas presented, the reader must make the only judgment or form the only ___(2)___ allowed by the facts. There should be no doubt about which conclusion the author expects you to reach.

3. Making Inferences. Unlike a conclusion, an inference is a reasonable judgment based on the facts. The idea you infer may not be the only one suggested, but it will clearly be the one the author ___(3)___ . Making inferences is one of the most critical areas of comprehension demanded of the reader.

4. Predicting Outcomes. Authors use ideas to ___(4)___ the reader to certain ends or objectives. The outcome may not be disclosed outright, but authors also provide a groundwork of the facts you need to predict the intended ___(5)___ .

5. Making a Judgment. Sometimes the author expects readers to make a judgment suggested by the facts and arguments.

6. Recognizing Tone. Finally, we are expected to demonstrate a sensitive appreciation and ___(6)___ of the author's work. We do that by recognizing tone—reacting to the joy or sadness of the article. We also understand and identify with characters. Finally, we visualize the realness the author has strived to ___(7)___ , and we see humor—and are moved to laughter—when that has been the goal.

(1)	found	appreciated	
	hinted	understood	stated
(2)	opinion	principle	
	index	illustration	graph
(3)	discarded	denied	
	intended	interrupted	interposed
(4)	lead	lend	
	discourage	follow	divert
(5)	collapse	result	
	success	behavior	record
(6)	dislike	criticism	
	awareness	fear	hatred
(7)	destroy	create	
	imitate	overcome	employ

Study Skills, Part Two—Read the study skills passage again, paying special attention to the lesson being taught. Then, without looking back at the passage, complete each sentence below by writing in the missing word or words. Check the Answer Key on page 108 for the answers to Study Skills, Part One, and Study Skills, Part Two.

1. Interpretation requires the most use of _____ from the reader.

2. The facts presented by the author allow only one _____ to be reached.

3. The idea you infer may not be the only one _____ .

4. The author lays a groundwork of facts from which the reader can _____ the outcome.

5. Reacting to the joy or sadness of a story is recognizing _____ .

Answer Key

Selection 1

Vocabulary

1. C
2. B
3. E
4. A
5. D
6. B
7. E
8. A
9. D
10. C

Comprehension

1. b
2. a
3. d
4. a
5. c
6. c
7. b
8. a
9. c
10. d

Study Skills, Part One

1. question
2. important
3. approach
4. plan
5. places
6. supporting
7. field

Study Skills, Part Two

1. Preview
2. scout
3. picture
4. examples
5. organize

Selection 2

Vocabulary

1. E
2. C
3. A
4. E
5. D
6. B
7. C
8. B
9. A
10. D

Comprehension

1. a
2. c
3. a
4. b
5. d
6. d
7. d
8. d
9. c
10. c

Study Skills, Part One

1. aware
2. arguments
3. information
4. humor
5. shock
6. interest
7. content

Study Skills, Part Two

1. reading the titles
2. feelings
3. titles
4. digest
5. words

Selection 3

Vocabulary

1. E
2. C
3. A
4. E
5. D
6. A
7. B
8. C
9. D
10. B

Comprehension

1. b
2. c
3. b
4. a
5. b
6. a
7. b
8. a
9. b
10. c

Study Skills, Part One

1. reader
2. written
3. set
4. end
5. author
6. learn
7. facets

Study Skills, Part Two

1. introduction
2. setting
3. important
4. summarize
5. skim

Selection 4

Vocabulary

1. E
2. A
3. C
4. B
5. D
6. A
7. D
8. E
9. C
10. B

Comprehension

1. d
2. b
3. b
4. a
5. b
6. a
7. a
8. d
9. c
10. b

Study Skills, Part One

1. inquiring
2. activity
3. prereading
4. outline
5. technique
6. expects
7. create

Study Skills, Part Two

1. ask questions
2. learn
3. presentation
4. contrast
5. following

Selection 5

Vocabulary

1. A
2. D
3. C
4. B
5. C
6. E
7. B
8. D
9. E
10. A

Comprehension

1. a
2. a
3. c
4. b
5. a
6. d
7. c
8. a
9. b
10. c

Study Skills, Part One

1. time
2. interfering
3. really
4. quiz
5. enough
6. works
7. best

Study Skills, Part Two

1. problems
2. attention
3. Motivation
4. goal
5. distractions

Selection 6

Vocabulary

1. E
2. C
3. E
4. B
5. A
6. D
7. C
8. D
9. A
10. B

Comprehension

1. d
2. b
3. a
4. c
5. a
6. c
7. d
8. c
9. a
10. a

Study Skills, Part One

1. finishes
2. challenge
3. clock
4. periods
5. complete
6. unfinished
7. related

Study Skills, Part Two

1. time
2. shorter
3. spread
4. tasks
5. list

Selection 7

Vocabulary

1. D	6. A
2. C	7. B
3. A	8. E
4. B	9. C
5. D	10. E

Comprehension

1. d	6. d
2. a	7. a
3. c	8. c
4. a	9. b
5. a	10. a

Study Skills, Part One

1. employ	6. facts
2. introduced	7. minimize
3. want	
4. entire	
5. questions	

Study Skills, Part Two

1. plan
2. tried
3. review
4. previewing
5. Generalize

Selection 8

Vocabulary

1. E	6. A
2. A	7. E
3. C	8. D
4. D	9. B
5. B	10. C

Comprehension

1. a	6. b
2. a	7. c
3. b	8. d
4. a	9. d
5. a	10. a

Study Skills, Part One

1. reader	6. places
2. introduced	7. important
3. appear	
4. value	
5. aware	

Study Skills, Part Two

1. obvious
2. letters
3. 4
4. beginning
5. summaries

Selection 9

Vocabulary

1. D	6. D
2. B	7. A
3. E	8. B
4. A	9. C
5. C	10. E

Comprehension

1. d	6. a
2. b	7. c
3. a	8. b
4. a	9. a
5. c	10. b

Study Skills, Part One

1. advance	6. identify
2. equal	7. alert
3. opposing	
4. previous	
5. similar	

Study Skills, Part Two

1. guide
2. difficult
3. forward
4. series
5. stronger

Selection 10

Vocabulary

1. C	6. A
2. B	7. E
3. A	8. D
4. E	9. B
5. C	10. D

Comprehension

1. d	6. d
2. a	7. c
3. b	8. d
4. d	9. c
5. b	10. b

Study Skills, Part One

1. urge	6. identify
2. job	7. statements
3. result	
4. pause	
5. meaning	

Study Skills, Part Two

1. new
2. specific
3. finished
4. textbooks
5. beginning

Selection 11

Vocabulary

1. E	6. B
2. C	7. D
3. A	8. C
4. E	9. A
5. B	10. D

Comprehension

1. a	6. b
2. c	7. b
3. d	8. c
4. d	9. d
5. b	10. a

Study Skills, Part One

1. important	6. intends
2. concluding	7. major
3. draw	
4. distinction	
5. subject	

Study Skills, Part Two

1. Terminal
2. end
3. new
4. finality
5. subject

Selection 12

Vocabulary

1. E	6. E
2. A	7. B
3. B	8. C
4. C	9. D
5. D	10. A

Comprehension

1. d	6. c
2. d	7. b
3. d	8. b
4. c	9. c
5. a	10. d

Study Skills, Part One

1. continuing	6. forward
2. direction	7. turn
3. different	
4. said	
5. significance	

Study Skills, Part Two

1. Counter
2. turnabout
3. lead
4. meaning
5. prepare

Selection 13

Vocabulary

1. A	6. B
2. E	7. E
3. D	8. C
4. C	9. B
5. A	10. D

Comprehension

1. b	6. a
2. c	7. a
3. c	8. b
4. a	9. d
5. d	10. b

Study Skills, Part One

1. well	6. opening
2. constructed	7. information
3. subject	
4. background	
5. reason	

Study Skills, Part Two

1. use
2. well organized
3. learn
4. practical
5. preface/introduction

Selection 14

Vocabulary
1. B	6. E
2. D	7. C
3. A	8. A
4. C	9. E
5. B	10. D

Comprehension
1. c	6. b
2. a	7. b
3. c	8. d
4. d	9. a
5. b	10. c

Study Skills, Part One
1. text	6. current
2. early	7. additional
3. presented	
4. background	
5. reference	

Study Skills, Part Two
1. organized
2. Historical
3. complex
4. preread
5. information

Selection 15

Vocabulary
1. A	6. C
2. D	7. B
3. E	8. E
4. A	9. C
5. B	10. D

Comprehension
1. c	6. a
2. b	7. c
3. c	8. a
4. d	9. c
5. d	10. c

Study Skills, Part One
1. name	6. powerless
2. topics	7. easier
3. evaluate	
4. checks	
5. opposite	

Study Skills, Part Two
1. subject
2. alphabetical
3. number
4. familiar
5. supplement

Selection 16

Vocabulary
1. E	6. C
2. A	7. D
3. B	8. C
4. D	9. E
5. B	10. A

Comprehension
1. a	6. b
2. d	7. d
3. c	8. a
4. a	9. b
5. c	10. c

Study Skills, Part One
1. wise	6. parting
2. limits	7. main
3. clue	
4. visual	
5. expected	

Study Skills, Part Two
1. organization
2. subheads
3. false
4. closing
5. skim

Selection 17

Vocabulary
1. A	6. D
2. E	7. B
3. C	8. B
4. E	9. D
5. A	10. C

Comprehension
1. c	6. a
2. d	7. c
3. b	8. b
4. b	9. d
5. c	10. a

Study Skills, Part One
1. own	6. pages
2. worthy	7. understand
3. unmarked	
4. mark	
5. important	

Study Skills, Part Two
1. creative
2. frequently
3. Brackets
4. number
5. abbreviations

Selection 18

Vocabulary
1. A	6. E
2. E	7. C
3. C	8. A
4. D	9. B
5. B	10. D

Comprehension
1. b	6. b
2. a	7. c
3. a	8. c
4. d	9. a
5. d	10. d

Study Skills, Part One
1. moving	6. parts
2. word	7. method
3. memorizing	
4. unfamiliar	
5. listening	

Study Skills, Part Two
1. mental
2. sight
3. recognize
4. phonics
5. analysis

Selection 19

Vocabulary
1. B	6. B
2. E	7. D
3. D	8. C
4. A	9. C
5. E	10. A

Comprehension
1. b	6. d
2. a	7. b
3. b	8. b
4. a	9. b
5. c	10. d

Study Skills, Part One
1. areas	6. first
2. remembering	7. facts
3. separate	
4. series	
5. classify	

Study Skills, Part Two
1. retention
2. organize
3. order
4. correct
5. generalizing

Selection 20

Vocabulary
1. D	6. A
2. C	7. E
3. A	8. D
4. B	9. E
5. C	10. B

Comprehension
1. b	6. b
2. a	7. d
3. d	8. b
4. c	9. a
5. a	10. c

Study Skills, Part One
1. stated	6. awareness
2. opinion	7. create
3. intended	
4. lead	
5. result	

Study Skills, Part Two
1. judgment
2. conclusion
3. suggested
4. predict
5. tone

Bibliography

Angelou, Maya. *The Heart of a Woman*. New York: Random House, 1981.

———. *I Know Why the Caged Bird Sings*. New York: Random House, 1969.

Baldwin, James. *Go Tell It on the Mountain*. New York: The Dial Press, 1953.

———. "Sweet Lorraine." In *To Be Young, Gifted and Black*, New Jersey: Prentice-Hall, Inc., 1969.

Baraka, Amiri. *The Autobiography of LeRoi Jones/Amiri Baraka*. New York: Freundlich Books, 1984.

Blay, J. Benibengor. "Funeral of a Whale." In *An African Treasury*. Edited by Langston Hughes. New York: Crown Publishers, 1960.

Brown, Claude. *Manchild in the Promised Land*. New York: The Macmillan Company, 1965.

Brown, H. Rap. *Die, Nigger, Die*. New York: The Dial Press, 1969.

Brown, Sterling. *The Massachusetts Review*. Amherst: University of Massachusetts, 1966.

Cade, Toni, Bambara. "The Pill: Genocide or Liberation." In *Onyx*. New York: Onyx Publications, 1969.

Carmichael, Stokely, and Charles V. Hamilton. *Black Power*. New York: Random House, 1967.

Clarke, John Henrik. "The Origin and Growth of Afro-American Literature." In *Negro Digest*. Chicago: Johnson Publishing Company, Inc., 1967.

———. "The Boy Who Painted Christ Black." In *American Negro Short Stories*. Edited by John Henrik Clarke. New York: Hill & Wang, 1966.

Cosby, Bill. *Fatherhood*. New York: Doubleday & Company, Inc., 1986.

Davis, Angela. *Women, Race and Class*. New York: Random House, 1981.

Douglass, Frederick. *The Narrative of the Life of Frederick Douglass*, 1845.

———. *What to the Slaves Is the Fourth of July?* 1852.

Dove-Danquah, Mabel. "Anticipation." In *An African Treasury*. Edited by Langston Hughes. New York: Crown Publishers, 1960.

DuBois, W. E. B. *Dusk of Dawn*. New York: Harcourt, Brace & World, 1968.

Dunham, Katherine. *A Touch of Innocence*. New York: Harcourt Brace Jovanovich, Inc., 1959.

Farmer, James. *Lay Bare the Heart*. New York: Arbor House Publishing Company, 1985.

Garvey, Marcus. *Philosophy and Opinions*, 1916.

Gregory, Dick, and Robert Lipsyte. *nigger*. New York: E. P. Dutton & Company, 1964.

Hansberry, Lorraine. *A Raisin in the Sun*. New York: Random House, 1958.

Hughes, Langston. " 'Tain't So." In *The Book of Negro Humor*. Edited by Langston Hughes. New York: Dodd, Mead & Company, 1966.

Jackson, Reggie, with Mike Lupica. *Reggie*. New York: Random House, 1984.

Jones, John H. *Harlem U.S.A.* New York: Seven Seas Publications, 1964.

King, Martin Luther, Jr. *The Trumpet of Conscience*. New York: Harper & Row, 1967.

Lindsey, Kay. *The Black Woman*. New York: New American Library, 1970.

Malcolm X and Alex Haley. *The Autobiography of Malcolm X*. New York: Grove Press, 1965.

Mandela, Nelson. "Indictment of South Africa." In *The Political Awakening of Africa*. New Jersey: Prentice-Hall, Inc., 1965.

Mandela, Winnie. *Part of My Soul Went with Him*. New York: W. W. Norton & Company, 1985.

Modisane, Bloke. "Why I Ran Away." In *An African Treasury*. Edited by Langston Hughes. New York: Crown Publishers, 1960.

Morrison, Toni. *Sula*. New York: Random House, 1973.

Oates, Stephen B. *Let the Trumpet Sound*. New York: Harper & Row, 1982.

Soyinka, Wole. *Aké: The Years of Childhood*. New York: Random House, 1981.

Terry, Wallace, Editor. *Bloods: An Oral History of the Vietnam War by Black Veterans*. New York: Random House, 1984.

Walker, Alice. "Brothers and Sisters" and "Choice: A Tribute to Dr. Martin Luther King, Jr." In *In Search of Our Mothers' Gardens*. New York: Harcourt Brace Jovanovich, Inc., 1983.

———. *The Color Purple*. New York: Harcourt Brace Jovanovich, Inc., 1982.

———. "The Diary of an African Nun." In *Freedomways*. New York: Freedomways Associates, Inc., 1968.

Walker, Margaret. *Jubilee*. Boston: Houghton Mifflin Company, 1966.

Washington, Booker T. *Up From Slavery*, 1900.

Wideman, John Edgar. *Brothers and Keepers*. New York: Henry Holt and Company, 1984.

Wilkins, Roger. *A Man's Life*. New York: Simon & Schuster, Inc., 1982.

Wright, Richard. *Black Boy*. New York: Harper & Row, 1945.

Vassa, Gustavus. *The Interesting Narrative of the Life of Oloudah Equiano, or Gustavus Vassa*, 1789.

Words per Minute

No. of Words	1585	1470	1265	1830	1435	1215	2060	2090	2040	2150	1555	1350	2095	1685	2010	1520	1875	1520	1430	1390
Selection	**1**	**2**	**3**	**4**	**5**	**6**	**7**	**8**	**9**	**10**	**11**	**12**	**13**	**14**	**15**	**16**	**17**	**18**	**19**	**20**
1:20	1220	1130	975	1405	1105	935	1585	1605	1570	1655	1195	1040	1610	1295	1545	1175	1440	1175	1100	1070
1:40	990	880	790	1145	895	760	1285	1305	1275	1345	970	845	1310	1050	1255	955	1170	955	890	870
2:00	790	735	630	915	720	605	1030	1045	1020	1075	775	675	1045	845	1005	765	935	765	710	695
2:20	690	630	550	795	625	530	895	910	885	935	675	585	910	735	875	665	815	665	625	605
2:40	610	550	485	705	550	465	790	805	785	825	600	520	805	650	775	590	720	590	550	535
3:00	560	490	420	610	480	405	685	695	680	715	520	450	700	565	670	510	625	510	480	465
3:20	510	440	385	555	435	370	625	635	620	650	470	410	635	515	610	465	570	465	435	420
3:40	440	400	350	510	400	335	570	580	565	595	430	375	580	470	560	425	520	425	400	385
4:00	395	365	315	455	360	305	515	520	510	535	390	335	525	425	500	380	470	380	360	345
4:20	370	340	295	425	335	280	480	485	475	500	360	315	485	395	465	355	435	355	335	325
4:40	345	315	275	395	310	265	445	455	445	465	340	295	455	370	435	330	405	330	310	300
5:00	315	295	255	365	285	245	410	420	410	430	310	270	420	340	400	305	375	305	285	280
5:20	300	275	240	345	270	230	390	395	385	405	295	255	395	320	380	290	355	290	270	260
5:40	285	260	225	325	255	215	365	375	365	385	275	240	375	300	360	275	335	275	255	250
6:00	265	245	210	305	240	200	345	350	340	360	260	225	350	280	335	255	310	255	240	230
6:20	250	230	200	290	225	190	325	330	325	340	245	215	330	270	320	240	295	240	225	220
6:40	240	220	190	275	215	185	310	315	310	325	235	205	315	255	305	230	285	230	215	210
7:00	225	210	180	260	205	175	295	300	290	305	220	190	300	240	285	220	265	220	205	200
7:20	215	200	175	250	195	165	280	285	280	295	215	185	285	230	275	210	255	210	195	190
7:40	210	190	165	240	190	160	270	275	270	280	205	175	275	225	265	200	245	200	190	180
8:00	200	185	160	230	180	150	255	260	255	270	195	170	260	210	250	190	235	190	180	175
8:20	190	175	150	220	170	145	250	250	245	260	185	160	250	205	240	185	225	185	170	165
8:40	185	170	145	210	165	140	240	245	235	250	180	155	245	195	235	175	220	175	165	160
9:00	175	165	140	205	160	135	230	230	225	240	170	150	230	190	225	170	210	170	160	155
9:20	170	160	135	195	155	130	220	225	220	230	165	145	225	180	215	165	200	165	155	150
9:40	165	150	130	190	150	125	215	215	210	225	160	140	215	175	210	160	195	160	150	145
10:00	160	145	125	185	145	120	205	210	205	215	155	135	210	170	200	155	185	155	145	140
10:20	155	140	120	175	140	115	200	200	200	210	150	130	205	165	195	150	180	150	140	135
10:40	150	135	120	170	135	115	195	195	190	200	145	125	195	160	190	145	175	145	135	130
11:00	145	135	115	165	130	110	185	190	185	195	140	120	190	155	180	140	170	140	130	125
11:20	140	130	115	160	125	105	180	185	180	190	135	120	185	150	175	135	165	135	125	125
11:40	135	125	110	155	125	105	175	180	175	185	135	115	180	145	175	130	160	130	125	120
12:00	130	120	105	150	120	100	170	175	170	180	130	110	175	140	165	125	155	125	120	115
12:20	130	120	105	150	115	100	165	170	165	175	125	110	170	135	165	125	150	125	115	115
12:40	125	115	100	145	115	95	165	165	160	170	125	105	165	135	160	120	150	120	115	110
13:00	120	115	100	140	110	95	160	160	155	165	120	105	160	130	155	115	145	115	110	105
13:20	120	110	95	135	105	90	155	155	155	160	115	100	155	125	150	115	140	115	105	105
13:40	115	105	95	135	105	90	150	155	150	160	115	100	155	125	145	110	135	110	105	100
14:00	115	105	95	130	100	85	145	150	145	155	110	95	150	120	145	110	135	110	100	100
14:20	110	100	90	125	100	85	145	145	140	150	110	95	145	120	140	105	130	105	100	95
14:40	110	100	85	125	100	85	140	145	140	145	105	90	145	115	135	105	130	105	100	95
15:00	105	100	85	120	95	80	135	140	135	145	105	90	140	115	135	100	125	100	95	90

Minutes and Seconds Elapsed

Progress Graph

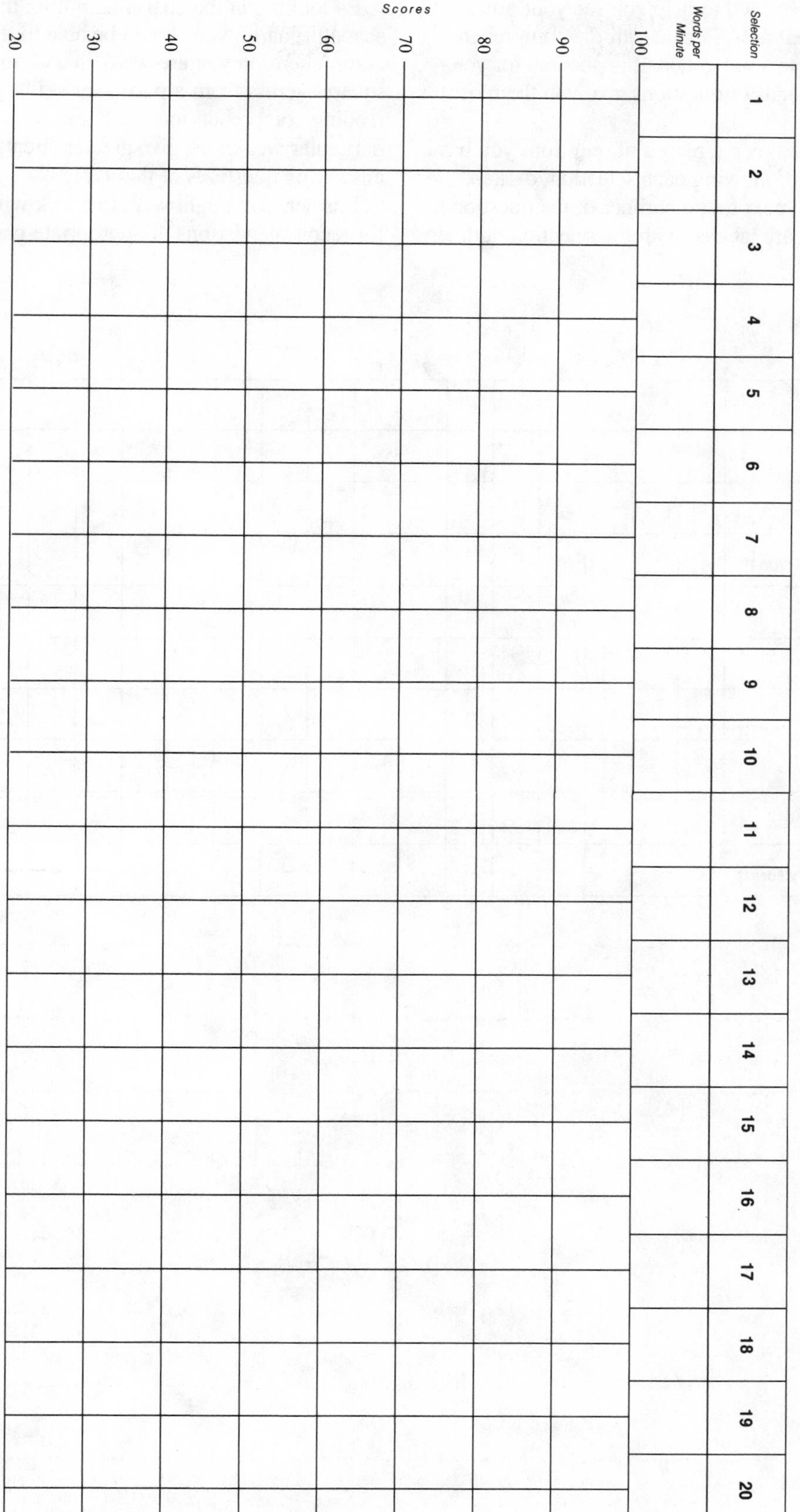
Selection
1
2
3
4
5
6
7
8
9
10
11
12
13
14
15
16
17
18
19
20
Words per Minute
Scores
100
90
80
70
60
50
40
30
20

Comprehension Skills Profile

The graph below is designed to help you see your areas of comprehension weakness. Because all the comprehension questions in this text are coded, it is possible for you to determine which kinds of questions give you the most trouble.

On the graph below, keep a record of questions you have answered incorrectly. Following each selection, darken a square on the graph next to the number of the question missed. The columns are labeled with the selection numbers.

By looking at the chart and noting the number of shaded squares, you should be able to tell which areas of comprehension you are weak in. A large number of shaded squares across from a particular skill signifies an area of reading comprehension weakness. When you discover a particular weakness, give greater attention and time to answering questions of that type.

Further, you might wish to check with your instructor for recommendations of appropriate practice materials.

Selection

Categories of Comprehension Skills	1	2	3	4	5	6	7	8	9	10	11	12	13	14	15	16	17	18	19	20
1. Recalling Specific Facts																				
2. Retaining Concepts																				
3. Organizing Facts																				
4. Understanding the Main Idea																				
5. Drawing a Conclusion																				
6. Making a Judgment																				
7. Making an Inference																				
8. Recognizing Tone																				
9. Understanding Characters																				
10. Appreciation of Literary Forms																				